# Making Good Law or Good Policy?

Raymond V. Carman, Jr.

# Making Good Law or Good Policy?

## The Causes and Effects of State Supreme Court Judges' Role Orientations

Springer

Raymond V. Carman, Jr.
Political Science
State University of New York College
at Plattsburgh
Plattsburgh, NY
USA

ISBN 978-3-319-53380-3 ISBN 978-3-319-53381-0 (eBook)
DOI 10.1007/978-3-319-53381-0

Library of Congress Control Number: 2017932080



Printed on acid-free paper

This Springer imprint is published by Springer Nature
The registered company is Springer International Publishing AG
The registered company address is: Gewerbestrasse 11, 6330 Cham, Switzerland

*To my husband and my family, for their love, patience, and support, and in the memory of my mother, Judith Marie Carman, father, Raymond Vincent Carman, and grandmother, Mary Ann Carman.*

# Contents

# Chapter 1
# An Empirical Puzzle

There can be little doubt that, at least in the United States, a significant level of discretion accompanies the role of judge. As evidence, consider, for example, the writings of three prominent jurists. First, in a 1993 speech "What I Ate for Breakfast and Other Mysteries of Judicial Decision Making," U.S. Court of Appeals Judge Alex Kozinski (1993, 993) argues that the existence of Legal Realism and Critical Legal Studies[1] proves "that even the silliest idea can be pursued to its illogical conclusion." He continues, "As I understand this so–called theory, the notion is that because legal rules don't mean much anyway, and judges can reach any result they wish by invoking the right incantation, they should engraft their own political philosophy onto the decision–making process and use their power to change the way our society works." However, despite such biting language, Judge Kozinski (1993, 996) acknowledges, "[While] there are more or less objective principles by which the law operates, principles that dictate the reasoning and often the result in most cases… these principles are not followed by every judge in every case, and even when followed, there is frequently some room for the exercise of personal judgment."

Second, in an article cleverly titled, "What Am I, A Potted Plant? The Case Against Strict Constructionism," U.S. Court of Appeals Judge Richard Posner (1987, 24) issues an ominous warning: "To banish all discretion from the judicial process would indeed reduce the scope of constitutional rights… The U.S. Constitution is a mixture of specific and general provisions. Many of the specific provisions have stood the test of time amazingly well or have been amended without any great fuss… Many provisions of the Constitution, however, are drafted in general terms. This creates flexibility in the face of unforeseen changes, but it also creates the possibility of multiple interpretations, and this possibility is an embarrassment for a theory of judicial legitimacy that denies that judges have any right to exercise discretion."

[1] Critical Legal Studies is a "school of thought advancing the idea that the legal system perpetuates the status quo in terms of economics, race, and gender by using manipulable concepts and by creating an imaginary world of social harmony regulated by law" (Garner 2004, 404).

 
R.V. Carman, Jr., *Making Good Law or Good Policy?*,
DOI 10.1007/978-3-319-53381-0_1

The third, and possibly most emphatic pronouncement of the discretion that judges in the United States enjoy, was made by then–New York Court of Appeals Judge (and future–U.S. Supreme Court Justice) Benjamin Cardozo. Warning that "[t]here can be no wisdom in the choice of a path unless we know where it will lead," Cardozo (1921, 102) writes, "The teleological conception of his function must be ever in the judge's mind. This means, of course, that the juristic philosophy of the common law is at bottom the philosophy of pragmatism. Its truth is relative, not absolute." He continues,

> If you ask how he is to know when one interest outweighs another, I can only answer that he must get his knowledge just as the legislator gets it, from experience and study and reflection; in brief, from life itself. Here, indeed, is the point of contact between the legislator's work and his. The choice of methods, the appraisement of values, must in the end be guided by the like considerations for the the one as for the other. Each indeed is legislative within the limits of his competence. No doubt the limits for the judge are narrower. He legislates only between gaps…How far he may go without traveling beyond the wall of interstices cannot be staked out for him upon a chart. He must learn it for himself as he gains the sense of fitness and proportion that comes with years of habitude in the practice of an art…(1921, 113-114)

Perhaps preemptively responding to potential critics, Cardozo points out this contention is not as absurd as some might initially think. "There is in truth nothing revolutionary or even novel in this view of the judicial function. It is the way that courts have gone about their business for centuries in the development of the common law" (1921, 116). He concludes, "You may say that there is no assurance that judges will interpret the mores of their day more wisely and truly than other men. I am not disposed to deny this, but in my view it is quite beside the point. The point is rather that this power of interpretation must be lodged somewhere, and the custom of the constitution has lodged it in the judges" (1921, 135).

Given the decades of experience from which these noted jurists speak, and the high regard with which they are held, it seems reasonable to believe that there exists the discretion in the function of judging that they observe and (at least on some level) argue in favor of. Judicial discretion might best be thought of, as Judge Posner more recently wrote, as a 'zone of reasonableness.' He explains, "There is almost always a zone of reasonableness within which a decision either way can be defended persuasively, or at least plausibly, using the resources of judicial rhetoric" (Posner 2006, 1053). With the existence of such discretion, a question logically follows: What is this discretion a choice between?

## 1.1 The Conventional Wisdom

In his groundbreaking book *Judges and Their Audiences: A Perspective on Judicial Behavior*, Professor Lawrence Baum (2006) sums up the conventional scholarly wisdom on judicial decision–making by explaining that appellate court judges are motivated by making good law, making good policy, or making both.[2] Indeed, broadly speaking, over the last several decades, scholars of judicial decision–making have, mostly, coalesced around the belief that an appellate judge's decision in any given case is the product of legal influences, attitudinal preferences, strategic considerations, or some combination thereof. Scholars have come to refer to these explanatory models as the legal model, the attitudinal model, and the strategic model, respectively.

The oldest of these models, the legal model, is rooted in the very founding of the English common law system. The theoretical foundations of the legal model are supplied by legal formalism, which is, as Judge Posner (1986, 181) describes it, "the use of deductive logic to derive the outcome of a case from premises accepted as authoritative." The legal model argues that, "in one form or another, decisions… are substantially influenced by the facts of the case in light of the plain meaning of statutes and the Constitution, the intent of the Framers, and/or precedent" (Segal and Spaeth 2002, 48). Despite these ancient roots, the legal model, Baum (2006, 8) notes, "maintains a foothold in law school teaching and exerts some influence on legal scholarship."

The legal model has been conceptualized in many ways and empirical investigations of the legal model have taken many forms. For example, Segal and Spaeth (1996) examine the extent precedent influenced the decision–making of U.S. Supreme Court justices who served on the Warren and Burger Courts.[3] To do so, the authors examine justices' votes in cases where the justices were presented with the opportunity to uphold a precedent that they had previously voted against establishing. If *stare decisis* matters, the authors contend, then justices who voted against establishing a precedent would, acknowledging that they are now bound by the precedent, vote to uphold said precedent in subsequent cases. The evidence is quite persuasive. In only 9.2% of the instances where justices were presented with the opportunity to uphold a precedent they voted against establishing did they actually do so. In other words, 90.8% of the time, justices continued to vote their preference against the original precedent.

Another conceptualization and empirical investigation of the legal model is provided by Collins (2008). Rejecting the argument that U.S. Supreme Court Justices "can robotically apply precedent and other legal rules to any given case to reach an objectively correct decision," Collins (2008, 83) instead conceptualizes the legal model as the influence amicus, or, friend of the court, briefs have on judicial decision–making. This legal persuasion exists "because it asks judges—consistent with their legal training and as unbiased decision makers—to endorse the position that is best supported by the tools of doctrinal analysis that make up the traditional legal model"

[2]While trial court judges might hold similar motivations, the additional burdens of fact–finding and appellate review certainly provide constraints on their behavior.

[3]The Warren Court began with Earl Warren's assumption of the chief justiceship on October 5, 1953 and ended with his retirement effective June 23, 1969. The Burger Court began with Warren Burger's assumption of the chief justiceship on June 23, 1969 and ended with his retirement effective September 23, 1986 (Epstein et al. 2012).

(2008, 84). He finds support for this conceptualization of the legal model. Collins (2008) concludes that amicus briefs are processed by the justices as persuasive communications that serve to persuade them to endorse the conclusions advocated in the briefs.

The attitudinal model and strategic model, on the other hand, are theoretically grounded in the legal realist movement of the early twentieth century. As Judge Posner (1986, 181) explains, legal realism is "deciding a case so that its outcome best promotes public welfare in nonlegalistic terms… A 'realist' decision is more likely to be judged sound or unsound than correct or incorrect [as a formalist decision might]." The attitudinal model, two of its biggest proponents, Segal and Spaeth (2002, 86), assert, "represents a melding together of key concepts from legal realism, political science, psychology, and economics. This model holds that the Supreme Court decides disputes in light of the facts of the case vis–à–vis the ideological attitudes and values of the justices."

Many scholars have explored the effect various measures of preference have on judicial decision–making. For instance, Segal and Spaeth (2002, 324), arguing that case facts are "juxtaposed against the attitudes of the justices in determining how any particular justice reaches a decision in any particular case," examine the effect that case facts and justices' ideology have on votes in search and seizure cases. The authors conclude that twelve case facts predict 62% of the justices' votes, ideology by itself predicts 70% of the justices' votes, and case facts along with ideology predict 71% of the justices' votes. The authors conclude, "one is clearly better off knowing the attitudes of the justices than the facts of the case" (Segal and Spaeth 2002, 325).

A second example of conceptualizing and analyzing the attitudinal model is provided by Sunstein et al. (2006). These authors examine the votes cast by U.S. Courts of Appeals judges to see if Republican appointees vote more conservatively than do Democratic appointees. If so, the authors conclude, judges' ideology must be influencing their decision–making. The authors find support for their contention: Republican appointees vote in a liberal direction only 48% of the time, while their Democratic–appointed brethren vote in a liberal direction 59% of the time.

Lastly, the strategic model holds that, while judges are motivated by their policy preferences, judges are not unrestrained actors and must therefore act strategically to secure the best possible, though probably not most preferred, outcome. This strategy manifests itself in many ways. An appellate court judge might join a more moderate opinion than he or she might prefer to ensure that a sub–optimal outcome prevails over the least–optimal outcome. A trial court judge might decide a particular case strategically so as not be be reversed on appeal. A court might, concerned about potential responses from another branch of government, dismiss a case rather than review it. Finally, a judge who is subjected to reelection might vote to sustain a defendant's conviction in order to appear tough on crime and thus secure their continuation in office.

Exploring the strategic model, for example, Epstein and Knight (1998) examine the opinion writing of U.S. Supreme Court justices during the 1969–1983 terms. The authors argue that wide–spread use of offers by a justice assigned to write a majority opinion to modify their opinion in order to secure the support of another justice (what the authors term 'bargaining statements') provides support of the strategic model. Examining the private papers of the justices, the authors find that one or more bargaining statements were made in 70.4% of landmark cases.

Another conceptualization and examination of the strategic model is provided by Brace and Boyea (2008), who explore the effect that public opinion on the issue of capital punishment has on both the composition of state high courts and state high court judges' voting. The authors find that in states where high court judges are elected, stronger public support for the death penalty produces a significantly more conservative bench and those judges are more likely to uphold a death sentence. No such relationships were found in states where judges are appointed by politicians.

Laudably, some scholars have sought to capture the influence all three explanatory models have on judicial decision–making. For instance, Pacelle et al. (2011) create an integrated model of U.S. Supreme Court decision–making that includes variables representing the legal model (precedent and issue evolution), the attitudinal model (the Court's ideology), and the strategical model (the policy preferences of the president and Congress). The authors find that in constitutional cases, the Court is unrestrained by external actors; instead, attitudes and law control judicial decision–making. However, in statutory cases, variables representing all three models are significant.

As Baum (2006) describes it, judicial discretion is a choice between making good law, making good policy, or making both. Indeed, scholars of judicial decision–making have mostly coalesced around the idea that an appellate judge's decision in any given case is a product of legal influences, attitudinal preferences, strategic considerations, or some combination thereof. There remains unanswered, however, an empirical puzzle implicit in that summary of judicial decision–making: What causes one judge to value legal influences more so than their attitudinal preferences? Or, said another way: Why do some judges value good law more so than good policy? Answering this puzzle is the motivation behind this work.

## 1.2 Summary of the Arguments

To answer this puzzle, the theoretical foundations of this work are based in the interdisciplinary concept of *role*.[4] Role theory, which draws on the disciplines of anthropology, business management, psychology, and sociology, is compelling for both its simplicity and intuitiveness. At its most basic level, role theory holds that how a person conceives his or her position affects how he or she performs in that position. Role theory's intuitiveness comes from its broad applicability and its pervasiveness. Each of us occupy many positions throughout our lives. Some of these positions are social, such as the position of child, friend, parent, or spouse. Others are professional, like the position of doctor, lawyer, judge, or professor. For each position we hold,

[4] For an extensive discussion of role theory, including its use broadly in the social sciences and political science, see Chap. 2.

we construct a role orientation based upon the expectations we have for ourself, the expectations that others have for us, and the environment within which we operate. This role orientation, which varies from person to person and position to position, determines how we act within our position.

This work examines the role orientations of judges on state high courts, or what are sometimes colloquially referred to as state supreme courts. I chose these courts specifically because they provide three important, and unique, opportunities that a similarly designed study of other courts would not. First, state courts decide the vast majority of cases filed each year and,[5] of those, state high courts have the final say in nearly all.[6] This nearly eliminates any influence that fear of reversal upon appellate review would have on either the judges' role orientations or their decision–making. Second, while federal courts all operate under the same institutional structure, the differing structures in which state high courts operate enables me to examine the effect that institutional design has on judicial role orientations. Third, while the the U.S. Supreme Court has homogenized in recent years,[7] thus decreasing the amount of variation in the personal characteristics and professional experiences of U.S. Supreme Court justices, the same is not true of state high courts. This greater diversity allows me to explore the extent to which these factors affect the development of role orientations.

Following the precepts of role theory, I argue: (1) judges' role orientations vary; (2) the institutional structures within which judges operate and the background characteristics and professional experiences of judges influence the development of their role orientations; and (3) judges' role orientations affect their decision–making. However, there are several key assumptions, which, while they follow conventions in both the role theoretic literature as well as the judicial decision–making literature, should be made explicit.

---

[5]A recent study found that over 103 million cases are filed in state courts each year (LaFountain et al. 2012).

[6]Of course, those cases that raise a federal constitutional or statutory question may be appealed to the U.S. Supreme Court.

[7]The Court's membership has homogenized in at least three important ways: religion, education, and professional experience. Historically, the Court's membership has been overwhelmingly Protestant (Epstein et al. 2012, Table 4-3). The current Court has six justices (66.6%) who are Catholics and three justices (33.3%) who are Jewish (Epstein et al. 2012, Table 4-3). Nationwide, 23.9% of the U.S. population practice the Catholic faith and 1.7% practice Judaism (The Pew Forumon Religi on & Public Life 2008, 10).

In terms of education, as late as 2005, a relatively low 55.5% of the Court's population were graduates from either Harvard Law School or Yale Law School (Epstein et al. 2012, Table 4-4). Today, eight of the current justices are graduates of either Harvard Law School or Yale Law School (Epstein et al. 2012, Table 4-4).

Finally, with the sole exception of Justice Elena Kagan, all of the current justices served on a U.S. Court of Appeals before joining the Supreme Court (Epstein et al. 2012, Table 4-9). Though historically speaking this was certainly not the case (see, e.g., Epstein et al. 2012, Table 4-9), it has now become the norm. That Justice Kagan had not previously served as a judge prior to her nomination to the Court was raised as a concern; "'My view is that her experience is very thin,' said Sen. Jeff Sessions (R-Ala.), the ranking Republican on the Senate Judiciary Committee, after an hourlong meeting with Kagan" (Oliphant and Mascaro 2010).

The first key assumption is that judges' role orientations vary. This assumption goes to the very heart of role theory. Over 100 years ago, scholars, searching for an explanation for how an individual becomes assimilated into society, began to piece together role theory. It began as a theatrical metaphor and evolved into the theory that an individual's performance in societal positions is determined "by social norms, demands, and rules; by the role performances of others in their respective positions; by those who observe and react to the performance; and by the individual's particular capabilities and personality" (Thomas and Biddle 1966). Given the differences in judges' personal characteristics and professional experiences, and the different structures within which each judge operates, it is reasonable to assume that judges will have varied role orientations. This assumption is supported by almost 60 years of studies on the judicial role orientation.

The second key assumption is that judges' role orientations fall on the 'restraintist–activist' continuum. Certainly the notion of 'restraintist' and 'activist' judges has been controversial in both the popular media as well as in the academic literature. The academic literature on judicial 'activism,' which has focused mainly on the U.S. Supreme Court, has taken two tracks: one normative, and the other empirical.[8] On the normative track, some scholars have argued that judicial 'activism' is bad[9]; others have argued that judicial 'activism' is good.[10] On the empirical track, some scholars have found support for judicial 'activism,'[11] while others have not.[12] All this aside, the most effectively measured and nearly universally accepted operationalization for the judicial role orientation is that of judicial 'activism.'

The third key assumption is that judges' role orientations affect their decision–making. As described in Chap. 2, following in the steps of Gibson (1977, 1978, 1981a, b, 1983), the judicial role orientation is conceptualized in this work as the stimuli that a judge feels can legitimately be allowed to influence his or her decision–making and, in the case of conflict among influences, what priorities to assign to different decisional criteria. Following logically from this conceptualization, the judicial role orientation has been operationalized in this work as falling on a continuum ranging from 'restraintist' to 'activist.' A 'restraintist' judge is a judge who believes that precedent, the strict construction of constitutions, and giving deference to legislative intent are extremely important decisional criteria. An 'activist' judge is a judge who gives greater decisional weight to personal attitudes, values, and case outcomes (Gibson 1983, 17–18). By definition then a 'restraintist' judge should vote to strike down legislation as unconstitutional less often than an 'activist' judge would, *ceteris paribus*, thereby having a direct effect on their decision–making.

---

[8]For a more thorough discussion of the academic literature on judicial 'activism,' see Chap. 2. For an excellent discussion of the history of judicial 'activism,' see Lindquist and Cross (2009).

[9]Some noted anti–judicial 'activism' scholars include Bickel (1962), Thayer (1893), and Tushnet (1999).

[10]Some noted pro–judicial 'activism' scholars include Barnett (1987), Bolick (2007), Miller (1982), and Peretti (1999).

[11]See, e.g., Casper (1976) and Mishler and Sheehan (1993).

[12]See, e.g., Dahl (1957).

## 1.3 Contribution to the Literature

While role theory provides a compelling tool with which to answer the puzzle motivating this work, my use is hardly its first. However, despite the existence of a voluminous literature, substantial opportunity remains for scholarship on the judicial role orientation.[13] First, much of the existing research examines trial court judges, not appellate court judges. The job of an appellate court judge is to decide, in a collegial context,[14] whether a legal error was made below. The job of a trial court judge is to preside at trial, provide instructions in jury trials, and issue rulings in bench trials. Given these significantly different jobs, attempts to leverage research on trial judges' role orientations to explain appellate judges' role orientations are less than optimal.

Second, the existing scholarship on appellate role orientations is not cross–institutional (e.g., the states studied use the same judicial selection method, the courts possess a similar degree of docket control, etc.). When a state legislature structures the state's judiciary, it does so to provide an environment within which the judges will operate. This design will promote behavior that is deemed favorable by the state and discourage behavior that is deemed unfavorable by the state. Therefore, studies that look at a single state or a small group of similar states are limited in their general applicability.

Third, much of the previous scholarship suffers from an inadequate conceptualization and/or operationalization of the judicial role orientation. Researchers often conceptualize role orientation as having a direct relationship with behavior. For instance, some have hypothesized that the only type of judicial 'activism' that exists is liberal 'activism,' thus dismissing the possibility that a judge might engage in 'activism' to achieve a conservative end. In addition, role orientation is almost always operationalized in such a way that there is little to no variation in the reported orientations.

Fourth, few attempts have been made to demonstrate the impact role orientations have on the decision–making process. Role orientations, like attitudes and strategy, only matter to the extent that they affect behavior. So, all things being equal, does a judge's role orientation affect the decisions the judge reaches? Scholars who have considered this question often use the judge's own reporting of his or her behavior, such as how often he or she overturns precedent. This subjective operationalization of judicial behavior is much less favorable than an objective observation of judicial behavior, like the one used in this work.

Finally, beyond merely providing an answer to an enduring puzzle in our scholarly understanding of judicial decision–making, this research is important because of the crucial role that state high courts play in American society. Far and away, Americans who have some interaction with our legal system, whether it falls under traffic law, family law, criminal law, civil law, etc., are most likely to have that interaction with a state court. The National Center for State Courts recently concluded that over 103 million cases are filed in state courts each year (LaFountain et al. 2012). In each of

[13] For a thorough discussion of the opportunities presented by the state of the existing literature, see Chap. 2.

[14] Or, said another way, on panels.

these states, of course, the state high court acts as the final arbiter of state law. Just in that capacity alone, state high courts are crucial. But, in addition, direct review by state high courts is asked in over 81,000 cases each year (LaFountain et al. 2012). Therefore, studies of these judges provide us insight not only into appellate judges and state high court judges, but also of judges who impact our daily lives.

## 1.4 Chapter Outline

Motivated by an enduring puzzle in our academic literature, this research answers three interesting and important questions. First: What are state high court judges' role orientations? Second: What causes these judges to develop particular role orientations? Third: What effect do these judges' role orientations have on judicial decision–making. To build the theory necessary to answer these questions, Chap. 2 begins by discussing role theoretic literature. I start by surveying role theory in the broader social sciences, before moving on to role theoretic studies within political science and of judicial behavior. Then I discuss the opportunities that exist to explore the judicial role orientation. The second half of Chap. 2 builds a theoretically–grounded conceptualization and operationalization of the judicial role orientation. Chapter 3 describes the ground–breaking survey of the entire population of state high court judges that was designed and implemented in order to gather the data necessary to answer these questions. Chapter 4 examines the extent to which institutional structure and judges' backgrounds affect the development of judges' role orientations. Closing the loop, Chap. 5 explores the effect judges' role orientations have on judicial decision–making. Finally, Chap. 6 provides some concluding thoughts, including a discussion of the implications of this work and potential for future research.

## References

Barnett, Randy. 1987. "Judicial Activism is Necessary." *Legal Times,* April 27.
Baum, Lawrence. 2006. *Judges and Their Audiences: A Perspective on Judicial Behavior*. Princeton: Princeton University Press.
Bickel, Alexander M. 1962. *The Least Dangerous Branch: The Supreme Court at the Bar of Politics*. Indianapolis: Bobbs-Merrill.
Bolick, Clint. 2007. "A Cheer for Judicial Activism." *Wall Street Journal,* April 3, A.15.
Brace, Paul, and Brent D. Boyea. 2008. "State Public Opinion, the Death Penalty, and the Practice of Electing Judges." *American Journal of Political Science* 52(2): 360–372.
Cardozo, Benjamin N. 1921. *The Nature of the Judicial Process*. New Haven: Yale University Press.
Casper, Jonathan D. 1976. "The Supreme Court and National Policy Making." *American Political Science Review* 70(1): 50–63.
Collins, Jr., Paul M. 2008. *Friends of the Supreme Court: Interest Groups and Judicial Decision Making*. Oxford: Oxford University Press.
Dahl, Robert A. 1957. "Decision-Making in a Democracy: The Supreme Court as National Policy Maker." *Journal of Public Law* 6: 279–295.

Epstein, Lee, and Jack Knight. 1998. *The Choices Justices Make*. Washington, D.C.: CQ Press.
Epstein, Lee, Jeffrey A. Segal, Harold J. Spaeth, and Thomas G. Walker. 2012. *The Supreme Court Compendium: Data, Decisions, and Developments*. 5th ed. Thousand Oaks: CQ Press.
Garner, Bryan A., ed. 2004. *Black's Law Dictionary*. 8th ed. St. Paul: Thompson West.
Gibson, James L. 1977. "Discriminant Functions, Role Orientations and Judicial Behavior: Theoretical and Methodological Linkages." *Journal of Politics* 39(4): 984–1007.
Gibson, James L. 1978. "Judges' Role Orientations, Attitudes, and Decisions: An Interactive Model." *American Political Science Review* 72(3): 911–924.
Gibson, James L. 1981a. "Personality and Elite Political Behavior: The Influence of Self Esteem on Judicial Decision Making." *Journal of Politics* 43(1): 104–125.
Gibson, James L. 1981b. "The Role Concept in Judicial Research." *Law & Policy* 3(3): 291–311.
Gibson, James L. 1983. "From Simplicity to Complexity: The Development of Theory in the Study of Judicial Behavior." *Political Behavior* 5(1): 7–49.
Kozinski, Alex. 1993. "What I Ate for Breakfast and Other Mysteries of Judicial Decision Making." *Loyola of Los Angeles Law Review* 26: 993–999.
LaFountain, Robert C., Richard Y. Schauffler, Shauna M. Strickland, and Kathryn Holt. 2012. *Examining the Work of State Courts: An Analysis of 2010 State Court Caseloads*. Washington, D.C.: National Center for State Courts.
Lindquist, Stefanie A., and Frank B. Cross. 2009. *Measuring Judicial Activism*. Oxford: Oxford University Press.
Miller, Arthur Selwyn. 1982. "In Defense of Judicial Activism." In *Supreme Court Activism and Restraint*, ed. Stephen C. Halpern, and Charles M. Lamb. Lexington: Lexington Books.
Mishler, William, and Reginald S. Sheehan. 1993. "The Supreme Court as a Countermajoritarian Institution?: The Impact of Public Opinion on Supreme Court Decisions." *American Political Science Review* 87(1): 87–101.
Oliphant, James, and Lisa Mascaro. 2010. "Supreme Court Nominee Kagan's Experience Questioned." *Los Angeles Times,* May 12.
Pacelle, Jr., Richard L., Brett W. Curry, and Bryan W. Marshall. 2011. *Decision Making by the Modern Supreme Court*. Cambridge: Cambridge University Press.
Peretti, Terri Jennings. 1999. *In Defense of a Political Court*. Princeton: Princeton University Press.
Posner, Richard A. 1986. "Legal Formalism, Legal Realism, and the Interpretation of Statutes and the Constitution." *Case Western Reserve Law Review* 37(2): 179–217.
Posner, Richard A. 1987. "What Am I, A Potted Plant? The Case Against Strict Constructionism." *The New Republic* September 28.
Posner, Richard A. 2006. "The Role of the Judge in the Twenty-First Century." *Boston University Law Review* 86(5): 1049–1068.
Segal, Jeffrey A., and Harold J. Spaeth. 1996. "The Influence of Stare Decisis on the Votes of United States Supreme Court Justices." *American Journal of Political Science* 40(4): 971–1003.
Segal, Jeffrey A., and Harold J. Spaeth. 2002. *The Supreme Court and the Attitudinal Model Revisited*. Cambridge: Cambridge University Press.
Sunstein, Cass R., David Schkade, Lisa M. Ellman, and Andres Sawicki. 2006. *Are Judges Political?: An Empirical Analysis of the Federal Judiciary*. Washington, D.C.: Brookings Institution.
Thayer, James Bradley. 1893. "The Origin and Scope of the American Doctrine of Constitutional Law." *Harvard Law Review* 7: 129–156.
The Pew Forum on Religion & Public Life. 2008. "U.S. Religious Landscape Survey." http://religions.pewforum.org/affiliations (March 6, 2013).
Thomas, Edwin J., and Bruce J. Biddle. 1966. "The Nature and History of Role Theory." In *Role Theory: Concepts and Research*, ed. Bruce J. Biddle, and Edwin J. Thomas. New York: John Wiley & Sons.
Tushnet, Mark. 1999. *Taking the Constitution Away from the Courts*. Princeton: Princeton University Press.

# Chapter 2
# The Judicial Role Orientation

This work offers a theoretically grounded and empirically tested answer to an enduring puzzle in the study of judicial behavior: Why are some judges motivated by what they see as good law while other judges are motivated by what they see as good policy? Though this work is specifically concerned with judicial decision–making, it follows from a puzzle ever present in the social sciences: Why do individuals who occupy the same position behave differently? To inform theoretical development, this chapter begins by speaking about this larger puzzle and attempts by other social scientists to answer it. Next, puzzles within political science are discussed, first from the field of legislative politics and then within the field of immediate interest, judicial politics. Finally, adopting and building on the extant literature, the chapter offers a theoretical framework to answer this puzzle of judicial behavior.

## 2.1 Role Theoretic Literature

### *2.1.1 Broader Social Sciences*

An ever present question in the social sciences is why individuals who occupy the same position behave differently. A very simple and compelling explanation is offered by role theory. Deriving its theoretical foundations from the literatures of anthropology, social psychology, and sociology, role theory provides that behavior is the product of (1) the environment in which an individual operates and (2) what the individual, as well as other relevant actors, define as position–appropriate behavior. This section provides crucial context for the instant study by chronicling some attempts by scholars from other disciplines to craft role theoretic explanations of social phenomena.

In research on higher education, for example, Rosch and Reich (1996, 115–116) study how "different academic disciplinary subcultures selected, socialized, and expressed institutional culture to new faculty, and the degree to which



R.V. Carman, Jr., *Making Good Law or Good Policy?*,
DOI 10.1007/978-3-319-53381-0_2

professional identity and role orientation were carried over, or adjusted, during the entry period." To explain these phenomena, the authors construct a four–stage theoretical model that includes: (1) the prearrival stage, which deals with a new faculty member's predispositions prior to entering their new position; (2) the encounter stage, which deals with a new faculty member's preconceptions formed during the recruitment and selection process; (3) the adaptation stage, which deals with external socialization and the new faculty member's identification with the organization; and (4) the commitment stage, which deals with the extent to which the norms and values of the new subculture are assimilated by the new faculty member (1996, 116).

To test their theory, the authors collect both quantitative and qualitative data. The former come by way of a survey to the current faculty of three academic departments at a doctoral–granting institution that hired new, first–time tenure–track faculty members. These current faculty members were asked to "describe their perceptions regarding the institutional culture, the degree of similarity or differences of institutional ideology between subcultures, and the role orientation of current group members in each subculture" (1996, 119). The role orientations are identified by way of "observation, structured and open–ended interviews, and a log format for new faculty to record their affective and cognitive reactions during the entry period" (1996, 119).

Related to role orientation, Rosch and Reich (1996) find that, while self–reported professional values remained relatively constant from before the new faculty member started their position to after they started their new faculty position, role orientation shifted slightly as faculty assimilated to their new setting. The authors conclude that while professional values are acquired during graduate training, role orientations appear only to be tentatively formulated then. Said another way: New faculty members automatically adopt the professional values learned during graduate school, but do not automatically adopt the role orientation espoused in graduate school. Rather, new faculty members gradually formulate their faculty role orientation by weighing the "role orientation espoused in graduate school against [their] personal values" (1996, 124).

From the disciplines of organizational management and psychology, Scandura and Ragins (1993), for example, examine the effect that both biological sex and gender role orientation have on the development of professional mentoring relationships in the male–dominated occupation of certified public accounting. The authors define the gender role orientation in terms of a spectrum where by masculinity and femininity are on opposite ends and androgyny is in the middle. The authors hypothesize that individuals who identify as having a masculine or androgynous role orientation will be more likely to have a mentor than individuals who identify as having a feminine role orientation, and that gender role orientation will explain more variation in mentorship than will biological sex.

The data for their study comes from a mail survey sent to a random sample of 3,000 certified public accountants by the authors. The useable responses numbered 800. To measure role orientation, respondents were asked a short form of the Spence Personal

Attributes Questionnaire.[1] To identify mentorship, respondents were asked whether they had a working relationship that significantly affected their career mobility. If the respondents answered yes, they were then asked a battery of 20 statements meant to measure the effectiveness of their relationship with a mentor.

The authors find that, while biological sex is not related to mentoring, gender role orientation is. Individuals who describe themselves as having an androgynous role orientation report more mentorship than individuals with either feminine role orientations or masculine role orientations. The authors suppose that this result might be because self–identified androgynous individuals, "who display both masculine and feminine characteristics, may have the potential to benefit more from mentoring relationships than individuals who display either masculine or feminine attributes" (1993, 262). To explain these findings, the authors note that, according to existing theory, androgynous individuals have greater behavioral flexibility than masculine or feminine individuals, which may be a factor in the effectiveness of mentor relationships. "Individuals with masculine orientations may be too independent, and therefore unable to accept their mentor's advice. On the other hand, proteges with feminine orientations can be overly dependent on their mentors, and may view their mentors as 'career saviours.' Androgynous proteges may be optimally suited for mentoring relationships in that they may have the flexibility to accept their mentor's help without becoming overly dependent" (1993, 262).

Also from organizational management and psychology, Shivers-Blackwell (2004) offers an explanation for why managers with similar jobs within similar organizations exhibit different leadership behaviors. She argues that people experience organizational role expectations and role pressures differently, which leads to the utilization of different leadership behaviors within the same context. While she does not empirically test the propositions that she creates to explain this phenomenon, she does develop an empirically–testable theory for future researchers to deploy. Her theory maintains that managers who perceive their organization's culture as being transformational are more likely to use transformational leadership. Conversely, managers who perceive their organization's culture as being transactional are more likely to use transactional leadership.

Borrowing from the extant literature, Shivers-Blackwell (2004, 43) defines a transformational leader as one "who articulates a vision of the future that can be shared with peers and subordinates, intellectually stimulates subordinates, pays attention to individual differences among people, is likely to use personal resources including time, knowledge and experience, and serves as a coach, teacher and mentor." Conversely, she defines a transactional leader as one who "exchange[s] rewards contingent upon performance and use[s] positional resources in order to encourage desired behaviors" (2004, 43).

Lastly from organizational management and psychology, Parker (2007) explores how the flexibility in an employee's role orientation affects his job performance. She defines flexibility in role orientation as the extent to which "various problems

[1]For more information on the Spence Personal Attributes Questionnaire, see Spence (1984) and Spence and Helmreich (1978).

reflecting longer–term goals beyond one's immediate technical job (e.g., customer dissatisfaction, slow delivery times) would be of personal concern to them rather than 'someone else's concern'" (2007, 412). The author hypothesizes that the more flexible an employee's role orientation, the higher the employee's job performance reviews will be.

To test her hypothesis, Parker (2007) studies the assemblers at a medium–sized electronics company in the United Kingdom. Controlling for background characteristics and job satisfaction, she attempts to predict the job performance reviews of employees based upon the flexibility in their role orientation. Parker (2007) finds, as hypothesized, that the more flexible an employee's role orientation is, the more favorably the employee's job performance review will be.

Finally, from the discipline of psychology, Tarter et al. (1975), for example, examine the effect that social role orientation has on the lethality of suicide attempts. The authors define social role orientation as "the disposition to turn anger inward as opposed to either avoidance or acting out of hostility" (1975, 295). They hypothesize that the most lethal attempts at suicide would be attempted by those most severely depressed, "since this type of affective disorder is often associated with introjection of anger" (1975, 295).

To test this hypothesis, two groups of subjects are examined. The first group contains 50 individuals who were admitted to a hospital for attempting suicide. The second group contains 50 individuals who were admitted to a hospitalized for mental health issues, but had never attempted suicide. Both groups were asked three questions to ascertain their role orientations and a set of questions related to their mental health. The authors make interesting discoveries related to sex, but do not find a statistically significant relationship between role orientation and the lethality of suicide attempts.

Many scholars have leveraged role theory to explain the social phenomena they observe. The works discussed above provide a sample of the various applications of role theory from other disciplines and provide crucial context for the instant study. From the enculturation of new faculty members, to the effect gender role orientations have on professional mentoring, and finally to the effect social role orientation has on the lethality of suicide attempts, scholars have found role theory a useful tool to explain a wide range of human behavior. Such uses support the adaptability of role theory to the study of state high court judges.

## 2.1.2 *Political Science*

### 2.1.2.1 Studies in Legislative Politics: Comparative Context

Just as role theory has been widely used across the social sciences, role theory has been widely used in various fields of political science, particularly in the study of legislatures and judiciaries. First, in the field of comparative legislatures, Gherghina (2011), for example, examines the effect that party type and size have on the role orientations of members of parliament (MPs) elected just after the fall of the communist governments in Poland, Hungary, the Czech Republic, and Slovakia. These MPs are extraordinarily unique and important, because "acting in 'adolescent' parliaments and non–institutionalized political systems, [they] were given fundamental tasks, such as being asked to draft constitutions, set institutions, and enact laws" (2011, 45).

Gherghina (2011) defines the MPs role orientation as being either that of delegate, trustee, or politico. An MP with a delegate role orientation is one who emphasizes the opinion of their voters or their party as a priority. An MP with a trustee role orientation is one who emphasizes his or her own judgment. An MP with a politico role orientation is one who alternates on whose opinion to emphasize, depending on the context.

The data for the MPs' role orientations come from interviews conducted with 600 newly elected MPs after the fall of each country's communist government.[2] To measure role orientation, MPs were asked, "If an MP has to vote, but holds an opinion which is different from the one held by his parliamentary club, should he then vote in accordance with the opinion of the parliamentary club or should he follow his own opinion?" (2011, 51). The MPs could choose between three categories: 'parliamentary club,' 'own opinion,' or 'it depends.' MPs who chose the first category were classified as delegate, the second as trustee, and the third as politico.

Gherghina (2011) finds that members of parliament from newly emerged parties are more likely to be delegates of either their constituents or their party than members of parliament from continuing parties or revived parties. She also finds that MPs from small parties are more likely to have delegate role orientations than MPs from large parties and that MPs from large parties are more likely to have politico role orientations than are MPs from small parties.

Van Vonno (2012, 131) argues that the difficulty previous legislative studies have had in finding a significant effect of role orientation on legislators' behavior might be explained by "scholars' tendency to focus on the classification of legislators according to one role orientation in a given typology, leading to the oversimplification of what is acknowledged to be a complex phenomenon." To address this deficiency, she explores whether Dutch MPs specialize in a particular role orientation or switch between role orientations depending on the situations which they find themselves in.

For this study, van Vonno (2012, 122) adopts the executive–legislative relations role orientations created by King (1976), as applied by Andeweg (1997). Specifically, the role orientations are defined as: nonparty mode, wherein an MP views his or her job as that of a parliamentarian whose main task is to check and balance the government; interparty mode, wherein an MP views his or her job as that of a partisan party member who is loyal to the party; and crossparty mode, wherein an MP views his or her job as that of an advocate who focuses on representing a particular interest or issue area.

The data for the MPs' role orientations comes from the 1990, 2001, and 2006 Dutch Parliamentary Studies. Specifically, the MPs were asked, "What do you

[2]Communism fell in each of these countries in either 1989 or 1990.

consider the best description of executive–legislative relations in each of the following situations?" (2012, 123). The situations the MPs were presented with were: in general, in budget proceedings (or committee work for the 2001 survey), and with regard to affairs or reports from Parliamentary Committees of Inquiry. Van Vonno (2012, 131) hypothesizes that "the context of executive–legislative relations in general will generate responses coupled to the interparty mode, budget proceedings is associated with the crossparty mode, and the context of affairs or reports from the Parliamentary Committee of Inquiry invokes responses connected to the nonparty mode."

Findings indicate that, as time goes on, MPs tend to switch roles less often and instead trend towards adopting the interparty mode role orientation. These findings run contrary to what might have been assumed in the literature. As van Vonno (2012, 131) explains, "The decrease in the number of role–switchers between 1990 and 2006 is indeed impressive, especially considering Andeweg's (1997) proposition that role–switching would be more important than role specializing in the Dutch Parliament." Also of interest, she finds that when MPs adopt the nonparty mode role orientation, opposition MPs are more likely to adopt the interparty mode role orientation.

#### 2.1.2.2 Studies in Legislative Politics: American Context

In the field of American legislative studies, Wahlke et al. (1960), for example, examine the effect that state legislators' role orientations have on their relationship with interest groups. Wahlke et al. (1960, 205) argue that defining role orientations in accordance with legislators' perceptions of what constitutes legitimate, desirable, or harmful activity "by pressure groups or other factors, as well as their perceptions of the supposedly objective 'facts' about such activity, are not random or idiosyncratic opinions held independently by each legislator individually, but are opinions intimately associated with what Truman (1951) has called the 'influence of office' and Latham (1952) has called 'officiality'."

The authors operationalize legislators' role orientations toward interest groups as either: a facilitator, who has a friendly attitude toward interest groups and knows much about interest group activity; a resister, who has a hostile attitude toward interest groups and knows much about interest group activity; and a neutral, who either has no strong attitude toward interest groups or has little knowledge about interest group activity (or both).

The data for the legislators' role orientations come from the 1957 survey responses of 474 legislators from four states.[3] Specifically, legislators were asked four questions: "Would you say that, on the whole, the legislature would work [better or worse] if there were no interest groups or lobbies trying to influence legislation? [Do you agree that] the job of the legislator is to work out compromises among conflicting interests? [Do you agree that] lobbyists and special interests have entirely too much influence in American state legislatures? [Do you agree that] under our form of

[3]The included legislatures were those of: California, New Jersey, Ohio, and Tennessee.

government, every individual should take an interest in government directly, not through interest group organizations?" (1960, 208). A role orientation scale was constructed by awarding the most interest group–friendly response four points, the second most interest group–friendly response three points, an undecided response two points, one point for responses on the unfriendly side of undecided, and zero points for the most interest group unfriendly response.

Confirming their hypotheses, Wahlke et al. (1960, 216) find that "facilitators are more likely to be aware of the nature of group demands and respond to them; resisters to be aware of them but deliberately fail to respond; neutrals to respond or resist, but for assorted other reasons, without caring or without knowing that a demand has been made by a group." Interestingly, in a tangential finding, the authors demonstrate that facilitators are significantly more likely to feel themselves to be effective legislators than are resisters or neutrals, and, while neutrals rank lowest of the three types in actual effectiveness, resisters rank lowest in sense of effectiveness.

Next, Prewitt et al. (1966, 569) challenge conventional wisdom that "adult political behavior is little more than an elaboration of patterns rooted in childhood experiences." To test the validity of this conventional wisdom, Prewitt et al. (1966) examine the role orientations of state legislators and city council members to determine whether those who became interested in politics at or prior to college have different role orientations than those who became interested in politics after college.

The authors define these legislators' role orientations in terms of representation, acceptance of interest group participation in the legislative politics, and how they formulate the job of lawmaker. For the representative role orientation, Prewitt et al. (1966) use the trustee, delegate, and politico designations. Interest group acceptance is defined in terms of: facilitators, who respond to and even seek out spokesmen for collective interests; neutrals, who occupy a more cautious but not necessarily hostile spot; and resisters, who view themselves as rejecting group demands. The final role orientation is operationalized as: inventor, who emphasizes policy initiation and innovative solutions to community problems; broker, who defines the legislator's function as compromising, arbitrating, and integrating differences; tribune, who expresses the will of the people; and the ritualist, who stresses the mechanisms of the legislative process and the mechanics of the legislator's job.

The data for the study comes from survey responses of 421 state legislators and of 129 city council members.[4] The survey wording for the role orientation questions is not provided. For the independent variable capturing when a legislator became interested in politics, survey respondents were asked, "How did you become interested in politics? For example, what is your earliest recollection of being interested in it? What other members of your family or close relatives held public or political office before you yourself did?" (1966, 572). This response was then categorized as: childhood or grammar school, adolescence or high school, college or equivalent period, after college or equivalent period, at time of entry into public life.

[4]The included state legislatures were those of: California, New Jersey, Ohio, and Tennessee. The cities analyzed were not identified.

The authors find early political socialization unrelated to major aspects of legislators' role orientations. They conclude, "[D]ifferences in orientations toward significant actors in the legislative arena and differences in self–evaluations are not rooted in experiences associated with the genesis of the political career" (1966, 581). The authors go on to posit, "A counter–hypothesis can be suggested: Intervening between initial political socialization and incumbent behavior are political experiences that condition subsequent behavior irrespective of factors associated with initial socialization. These experiences interrupt the career sequence and retard or even reverse patterns formed during earlier stages" (1966, 581).

Hadley (1977, 309) criticizes the state of the legislative role orientation literature: "Despite heavy investment of research effort in legislative role orientations, political scientists have produced scant evidence that role orientations are related to observable behavior." To remedy this deficiency, he creates a multidimensional role orientation and examines the relationship between this role orientation and roll–call voting behavior in the Indiana House of Representatives.

The four dimensions of Hadley's (1977) role orientations are: party, separation of powers, style, and areal focus of representation. For party role orientation, he classifies legislators as strongly pro–party, moderately pro–party, and party neutral. The separation of powers role orientation classifies legislators as those favoring strict separation between governor and legislature, moderate separation between governor and legislature, and favorable to gubernatorial involvement in the legislative process. The style role orientation represents the traditionally–defined legislative role orientation: trustee, politico, and delegate. Lastly, the areal focus role orientation captures whether the legislator views his or her relevant constituents as residents of the district, residents of the state, or both.

Role orientation data and the data needed for other independent variables for Hadley's (1977) study comes from interviews conducted in 1969 with members of the Indiana House of Representatives. An impressive 99 out of 100 of the Indiana House members were interviewed and a total of 11 questions were asked to capture legislators' views on the appropriate level of influence the party and the governor should have on legislators and the legislators' own views about who they represent. The decisional dependent variable comes from the roll–call votes of House members on all bills for which the author could identify either party position or gubernatorial position.

Hadley (1977) finds that the role orientations toward party, separation of powers, style, and areal focus of representation are correlated with legislators' support for party and gubernatorial positions. However, when these role orientations are entered into a multiple regression analysis with control variables, the significance of role orientations diminishes greatly. An interesting distinction appears in the difference in effect role orientations have on members of the majority and minority: role orientations appear to be more important among the minority Democratic legislators than they do the majority Republican legislators. The authors speculate that the pressure of party may be sufficient to overcome the role orientations of majority party members because the majority party stands a good chance of being able to enact its preferred policy and create a record for itself.

#### 2.1.2.3 Studies in Judicial Politics: Comparative Context

Finally though the focus of this study is on the role orientations of state high court judges, it is useful to explore some studies of the role orientations of other judges. In the field of comparative courts, Flango et al. (1975, 278), for example, examine the role orientations of European appellate judges "in order to begin clarifying some... ambiguities" around the judicial role orientation. Particularly, the authors argue that, instead of only thinking of judges' role orientations in terms of adherence to precedent, we should rather consider "at least two clearly distinguishable dimensions: judges' orientation toward precedent, and toward the public they serve" (1975, 277).

The data for the study comes from a mail survey of 238 German–speaking mid–level appellate judges in Austria and Switzerland during the fall of 1972. The survey questions were borrowed from role theoretic studies of American judges and were converted into German "after lengthy discussions with European attorneys, judges, and law professors about the technicalities of translating the English questionnaire into German" (1975, 280). To measure the judges' role orientations, they were asked how influential several factors were to a judge when deciding cases. For the first dimension, the factors presented were: "1. Decisions closest in facts to the present case; 2. Past decisions of the supreme court; 3. Precedent, when clear and directly relevant; 4. Judges are merely instruments of the law and can will nothing; 5. It is possible for a judge always to be politically neutral and nonpartisan in deciding cases; and 6. Adherence to precedent must be the rule rather than the exception if litigants are to have faith in the continuity of law" (1975, 281). For the second dimension, the factors presented were: "1. What the public expects; 2. The social consequences of the decision; 3. Requirements of the social order; 4. Judges should use their knowledge of social and political factors, as well as the law, in making their decisions; 5. Through cases brought to the courts, judges must constantly balance conflicting interests in society; 6. It is important that judges keep in constant contact with changing social mores in order to make their decisions relevant to the community; 7. Judges' view of justice in the case; and 8. It is more important that judicial decisions be just than that the letter of the law be adhered to" (1975, 283).

Flango et al. (1975) conclude both dimensions appear to be present in judges' role orientations. The judges, the authors find, can be broken down into four ideal role types: First are the 'law appliers,' who rank precedent high, but are not concerned with the community. Second are the 'law extenders,' who rank both precedent and community high. Third are the 'mediators,' who rank both precedent and community low. Fourth are the 'policy makers,' who rank precedent low and community high. The authors find the 'law applier' role orientation to be the most prevalent. Indeed, 40% of the Austrian judges and 53% of the Switzerland judges identify as such. The authors compare these findings to similar studies and conclude that this high proportion of of 'law appliers' is not unique to Austria and Switzerland, supposing "This may mean that Law Applier is the easiest judge to identify, both for researchers and for respondents, since it does appear to represent the 'ideal' judicial role" (1975, 285).

Likewise in comparative politics, Itoh (2010, 239) explores Japanese Supreme Court justices' perceptions of their role orientation as a lens through which to view their "attitudes toward elitist governance." He defines role orientation in terms of the Japanese Supreme Court's agreement with the political branches of government on constitutional issues and operationalizes the justices' role orientations in terms of a two–by–two approach to judicial activism and judicial restraint. A Court is seen as activist, as Itoh (2010, 242–243) defines it, "if it changed the existing judicial precedent while the political branch stood pat," "where conflict occurred due to a change of policies by law–makers while the judicial precedent remained unchanged," or "if both sides changed their policies at different paces or in different directions." A Court is seen as restraintist, on the other hand, when it adheres to its own precedent or "when it changes its existing judicial precedent while policy–makers also change their policies in such a way that both sides agree on the direction and pace of a change" (2010, 242).

The data for this study comes from a doctrinal case analysis of cases decided by the three petty benches of the modern Japanese Supreme Court.[5] Itoh (2010) finds that the Japanese Supreme Court was occasionally activist in the early days of its existence. Beginning in the mid–1970s, however, the Japanese Supreme Court became restraintist on 'law and order' and labor rights issues. He concludes, "The Court became rigidly pro–government and maintained harmony with the conservative government not because the Court was powerless and subservient but because of the shared values of governance regarding the primacy of national security, public welfare and corporate capitalism" (2010, 272).

#### 2.1.2.4 Studies in Judicial Politics: Federal Context

In terms of the U.S. Supreme Court, James (1968, 160) seeks to answer the question "How far does the Court form the Justice's conception of his role, and how far is that conception formed by his previous experience and opinions." James (1968, 162) sees a role theoretic explanation of particular value because of "its ability to bridge the dichotomy between structural and behavioral elements" and thereby define "a set of structural and behavioral elements [that] can be organized to specific aspects of the judicial role set."

Adopting a case–study approach, James (1968) considers the justices appointed by Franklin Roosevelt because, "Prior to their appointment, these men had been active, vocal supporters of the New Deal. They had experienced the frustration of their legislative goals... Their involvement thus invited the development of explicit judicial philosophies prior to their accession to the Court" (1968, 162–163). Of the eight Roosevelt appointees, James (1968, 163) decides to select Justices Robert

[5]These petty benches are similar to the appellate panels of the U.S. Courts of Appeals in that they are subsets of the entire bench. Any of the three five–member petty benches must forward a case to the grand bench in order to change judicial precedent, however (Itoh 2010, 244).

H. Jackson and William O. Douglas because they stood on opposite sides of the "spectrum of thought on the Supreme Court of their day."

James's (1968) data comes from the words of the justices themselves. She examined the two justices' unpublished speeches, published writings, and their judicial opinions. Justice Douglas was also personally interviewed. In addition, secondary materials were consulted including biographies of the justices, their colleagues, and contemporaries; interpretations of the justices' work; and memorial tributes to Justice Jackson (whose death preceded publication of the work).

James (1968) finds that role orientation led Justice Jackson to place greater emphasis on stability and continuity in the law. In contrast, Justice Douglas considered the values of flexibility and change more significant. James (1968) speculates that the justices' role orientations are products of their life experiences. "The entire pattern of Justice Douglas' life was one of reaching the desired conclusion over great odds by sheer force of will. When there was something desired, such as strong legs, or a trip to New York, or the protection of civil liberties, it had to be accomplished... Justice Jackson's comfortable rural background, wide and reflective reading, and experience at the Nuremberg Trials made him profoundly aware of the limitations of his own views as well as those of all men, and the significance of 'the safeguards of law so painstakingly built up in the course of the centuries" (1968, 184–185).

Next, Howard (1977, 917) confronts a vexing status quo: "Since the Supreme Court grants certiorari in less than 2% of federal appeals, internalized professional values have traditionally been regarded as essential controls binding federal courts into a system. Yet, the appropriate roles and functions of federal appellate judges have never been fixed nor universally accepted." To address this deficiency, Howard (1977, 918) explores "the relationships among judicial role perceptions and voting behavior in three leading intermediate tribunals—United States Courts of Appeals for the Second, Fifth, and District of Columbia Circuits—against a backdrop of the political orientations of their members."

Howard (1977, 918) defines the judges' role orientations in terms of the permissible range of discretion judges have in making law. He operationalizes judges' role orientations in terms of their function as law–makers. 'Innovators' are those judges who "felt obliged to make law 'whenever the opportunity occurs' (1977, 919)." 'Interpreters' are those judges who felt "judicial lawmaking should be held to a minimum" (1977, 920). Finally, 'realists' are those judges who took a middle position.

The data for Howard's (1977) study comes from off–the–record interviews conducted in 1969–1971 with 35 active and senior judges of the three circuit courts. Role orientations were inferred from the interviewees' "responses to open–ended and structured questions, including the following query concerning innovation: 'Some people think circuit judges should be legal innovators, thus illuminating issues for the Supreme Court; others argue that circuit judges should merely apply the law, leaving legal innovations to legislatures and the Supreme Court. What do you think?' (1977, 919). The dependent voting data was compiled by analyzing all decisions of the three courts decided between 1965–1967.

Howard (1977) finds that five judges were 'innovators,' 20 judges were 'realists,' and nine judges were 'interpreters.' Interestingly he notes, "that these federal circuit judges, unlike some members of state supreme courts, differed over issues of degree rather than of kind. Virtually all of them agreed that, while bold policy ventures such as *Brown v. Board of Education* (1954) should be left to the high court or Congress, *stare decisis* is 'not an unbreakable rule' (1977, 919)." Howard (1977) also finds moderate support for his proposition that 'innovators' are generally more libertarian in their voting behavior than are 'realists' and 'interpreters.'

#### 2.1.2.5 Studies in Judicial Politics: State Context

Scholars have explored the role orientations of state court judges for nearly fifty years. In one of the earliest works on the subject, Becker (1966) examines the impact of judicial role orientation upon judicial decision–making. To do so, 30 Hawaiian judges were surveyed, of which 22 responded. The judges were first asked to indicate, on a five–point scale, the influence each of seven factors had on the judge's decision–making process.[6] The judges were then asked to decide a hypothetical scenario involving a suit against a hospital claiming damages for the negligence of a nurse operating within the scope of her employment. The scenario was constructed in such a way that the 'objective' response, according to the author, was that the hospital should be absolved from liability.

When the survey results were combined with the judge's decision in the hypothetical scenario, Becker (1966) finds that judges who consider precedent to be the most important decisional factor are more likely to rule 'objectively.' Judges who do not consider precedent to be the most important decisional factor or who consider personal factors (their view of 'justice' or 'common sense') to be the most important decisional factor are more likely to rule 'subjectively.' This work improves upon Becker (1965), wherein the author used law students instead of judges to gauge the impact of role orientation on judicial decision–making.[7] Like much of the scholarship to follow, however, this study suffers from a lack of variation in role orientation responses:

> Over 90% of the judges in Becker's study rated 'precedent' as 'extremely' or 'very' influential, and the remaining two judges rated it as 'influential.' The variance of the responses to this item is smaller than the variance for any of the other items. Becker's analysis is based in part on dichotomizing the judges into two groups: those who rated precedent as 'extremely influential' and those who rated precedent as 'very influential' or as just 'influential.' This

---

[6]These factors were: (1) what the public needs, as the times may demand; (2) what the public demands; (3) the decision–maker's view of justice in the particular case; (4) common sense; (5) a highly respected lawyer as advocate; (6) a highly respected lawyer as an esteemed and/or influential member of the community; and (7) precedent, when clear and directly relevant.

[7]Surveying judges to gauge their role orientation is preferable to surveying law school students to obtain their best guess of how judges perceive their role orientation because law school students have no experience as a judge. Not having performed the job of judge affects the accuracy with which a law school student could describe the role orientation of judges.

> seems a rather artificial division point, one which is dictated by the lack of variance in the responses rather than by a theoretical concern…it seems possible that a great amount of within–group variance still exists (Gibson 1981b, 298).

Perhaps, as argues Gibson (1981b), a more significant problem with Becker's (1966) measure of role orientation lies in its lack of conceptualization. What does it mean to say that a judge is strongly oriented toward precedent? Becker (1966) essentially argues that relying on precedent is 'objective' while relying on some other factor is 'subjective.' Gibson (1981b) notes one further problem with the measure of role orientation: Becker's (1966) question requires a judge to determine how influential several decisional criteria *actually are* to the judge. However, "The proper form of the question, if it is to be used as a measure of role orientations, should express valuation of each of the criteria—the question should ask how influential the criteria *should be* [to the judge]" (Gibson 1981b, 299).

The next scholars to examine the judicial role orientation, Jaros and Mendelsohn (1967), attempt to determine what effect role orientation has on traffic court sentencing. The authors argue that, because the role orientation of judge includes the right to be respected, defendants who fail to demonstrate respect will receive a more severe sentence than defendants who are respectful. To conduct this study, secondary school teachers were trained and dispatched to observe the behavior of judges and defendants in Detroit Traffic Court for two weeks during the summer of 1966. The teachers were asked to observe the nature of the charges; disposition of the case; the sex, race, and age of the defendant; how the defendant was dressed; and whether the defendant failed to use an honorific title when addressing the judge, expressed disagreement, raised his or her voice, used sarcasm, expressed disparagement of the court or the police, or failed to express repentance.

The study concludes that, in low to moderately severe crimes, defendants who dress poorly are more likely to be jailed than defendants who dress well.[8] The defendant's demeanor, however, does not have a significant impact on jail sentences or fine magnitude. This research is compelling in that it deals with observed behavior: the disposition of cases by Detroit Traffic Court judges. It is limited, however, because of the same. As Gibson (1981b) explains, when the observed decisional behavior of judges is used to *infer* the existence of particular role orientations, the degree to which role orientations are related to behavior cannot be specified. "Indeed, the hypothesis that role attributes and behavior are unrelated cannot be tested. Nor can the relative impact of role orientations and other possible determinants of behavior be estimated" (1981b, 295).

Several years later, Ungs and Baas (1972) created a 'typology' of judicial role orientations by examining 120 articles authored by incumbent or retired judges, judicial opinions, and various other comments by judges in which a judge expressed an opinion about the judicial role orientation. From these, four role orientations

---

[8]The authors find no relationship between highly severe crimes and dress, or between dress and fine amount.

are created: (1) 'law interpreter,'[9] (2) 'law maker,'[10] (3) 'adjudicator,'[11] and (4) 'administrator.'[12] A sample of 48 statements used to create these role orientations was mailed to a random sample of 109 Ohio State judges. Each judge was asked to rate his or her agreement with the 48 statements on an 11–point scale. Fifty judges responded. Because no judge factored as a 'law maker,' the authors remove that category, though they identify two new role orientations from survey responses: 'trial judge'[13] and 'peacekeeper.'[14]

As suggested by previous studies, and in accord with the articulated views of judges,[15] the authors hypothesize that appellate judges will have a 'law maker' or 'adjudicator' role orientation and trial judges will have a 'law interpreter' or 'administrator' role orientation. This hypothesis receives only limited support: A greater proportion of appellate judges factor as an 'adjudicator' and a greater proportion of trial judges factor as a 'trial judge.' However, other differences among appellate and trial court judges do not emerge in the remaining role orientations.

This work is laudable in that it is the only study of appellate and trial judges that does not combine the responses of the two. However, several questions remain. Why did no judge identify as a 'law maker'? There are certainly reasons to believe that (at least) some judges act in ways that are comparable to law–makers. Motivated reasoning tells us that, since it is generally considered ethically or socially unacceptable for judges to say that they consider their role as that of law–maker, these judges might not publicly identify as such yet continue to act in a manner consistent with that of 'law maker' (Segal and Spaeth 1996; Braman 2009). Moreover, according to Gibson (1981b), this study is plagued with additional deficiencies. "First, a potpourri of 48 items, with enormously diverse content, was employed. Second, no attention was given to scale building: rather than R–analysis, the data were analyzed through Q factor analysis. This technique locates respondents, not scale items, in

[9]The 'law interpreter' believes that legal precedent should comprise the major criteria in judicial decisions and, consequently, advocates judicial self–restraint as a necessary control over reading personal predilections into law (Ungs and Baas 1972, 345).

[10]The 'law maker' argues that the acquired attitudes and experiences of a judge should be major factors in judicial decision–making (Ungs and Baas 1972, 346).

[11]The 'adjudicator' sees his or her job as that of "balancer of contending principles, evaluator of the conditions in society, and as a decision maker to achieve the welfare of society" (Ungs and Baas 1972, 347).

[12]The 'administrator' views his or her job as that of an executive. In order to administer justice, close attention must be paid to judicial procedures since procedures are as important to the judicial task as the decisions themselves (Ungs and Baas 1972, 347).

[13]The 'trial judge' feels his or her job is to interpret and carry out the decisions of higher courts (Ungs and Baas 1972, 358).

[14]The 'peacekeeper' perceives the role of the court "not only with reference to the results of particular cases, but also in terms of an activist in maintaining harmonious social relations" (Ungs and Baas 1972, 360).

[15]See, for example, Friend (1954), Martin (1945), and Medina (1963).

multidimensional space. Nevertheless, the authors discussed their results as if R–analysis had been conducted" (1981b, 300–301).[16]

In the first multi–state analysis of judicial role orientations, Wold (1974) interviewed 22 members of the Delaware, Maryland, New York, and Virginia high courts. In order to determine their role orientation, each judge was asked, "What do you think of the controversy over whether appellate judges should act as law interpreters or law–makers?" (1974, 239–240). Twelve responded that appellate judges should be 'law interpreters,' three that appellate judges should be 'law makers,' and seven that appellate judges should be some mix of the two. Each judge was then asked to identify his or her ideological predisposition before joining the court. Ten considered themselves to be 'conservative,' six were 'moderate,' and six were 'liberal.'

Next, the author asked about each judge's background (rural or urban upbringing, class, political party affiliation, religion, education, career background, age, and length of service). Wold (1974) finds that self–expressed ideology relates much more strongly to the judges' orientation toward judicial law–making than does social background characteristics or recruitment methods. This study is quite innovative in that it examines judges in different states and that it includes information about the judges' backgrounds.

However, one cannot put too much weight on the findings that background and institutional differences do not matter. These findings might very well be an artifact of the research design. The judges' role orientations were obtained through response to a single open–ended question, the use of which poses a serious threat to reliability. "Even though coding open–ended responses is a perilous task, intercoder reliability coefficients are rarely reported (and are somewhat disconcerting when they are reported). This approach also makes comparison across studies difficult, especially since there is no evidence that different researchers use a standardized set of coding instructions" (Gibson 1981b, 297).

Furthermore, like Becker (1966), both Ungs and Baas (1972) and Wold (1974) suffer from the use of a measure that yields little variation in the role orientations among judges. "Most studies have revealed that a majority of judges are 'law interpreters,' but it is extremely unlikely that judges are as homogeneous as the responses to this question make them appear. Instead there is probably substantial variation in the beliefs of 'interpreters' about what constitutes the proper bounds of 'interpretation,' variation which is critically important to understanding the decisions of the judges" (Gibson 1981b, 296–297). In other words, these studies operationalize role orientation in such a way that the category of 'law interpreter' captures judges who should be classified as something else.

In another study on criminal sentencing, Gibson (1977) examines the severity of the sentence received by defendants in 1,194 felony cases heard by the judges of the

[16]R–analysis, or normal factor analysis, finds correlations between variables across a sample of subjects. Q factor analysis, on the other hand, looks for correlations between subjects across a sample of variables (Kerlinger 1964, 581–582).

Superior Court of Fulton County, Georgia, between 1968 and 1970. For each case, seven non–legal variables were coded: (1) the defendant's race; (2) the defendant's sex; (3) the type of plea entered by the defendant; (4) whether the number of charges on which the defendant was convicted were reduced; (5) the length of time between arrest and trial; (6) whether the pre–trial period was spent in jail or on bail; and (7) an interactive variable that measured the pre–trial sanctions on the defendant (length of time between arrest and trial multiplied by pre–trial period in jail or on bail).

With these factors acting as independent variables and the defendant's sentence as the dependent variable, discriminant functions were calculated.[17] If the discriminant function is a good predictor of behavior, then the judge is considered an 'activist;' if the equation is not a good predictor, then the judge is considered a 'restraintist.' Gibson (1977) finds that, for five of the 11 judges studied, the seven non–legal stimuli explained 20% or more of the variance in sentencing behavior. Quite correctly, Gibson (1977, 999) notes that "while activism is a concept frequently associated with 'liberals' it may be very much more useful to think of the concept… [as] the ability of political or non–legal factors to explain variation in voting behavior."

This work, however, is not timeless. The cases under examination are from a trial court in Atlanta during the years 1968–1970. Sentencing behavior was picked because, at the time, judges were relatively unrestrained in sentencing defendants. Gibson (1977, 987) states, "A great deal of discretion is granted to trial court judges in sentencing; indeed, discretion is so great that some judges have bitterly complained about the lack of guidance for their decision." This is no longer the case. Much of judges' sentencing discretion has been replaced with legislative proclamations in the form of mandatory minimums, sentencing guidelines, and three–strikes laws.[18] This new reality surely has since been incorporated into the role orientation of judges and, as such, our operationalization of the judicial role orientation must evolve.

Gibson (1978) next attempts to determine the effect of both ideology and role orientation on trial court judges. To do so, he examines the sentencing behavior of 27 Iowa trial court judges in 2,715 felony or indictable misdemeanor cases filed during 1972 or 1973 and completed by 1974. Twenty–six of the 27 judges under investigation were interviewed. Ideology was determined by asking the judges to place themselves on the liberal–conservative spectrum and for their opinion about government economic intervention, class–based beliefs, and religious influence on society. Role orientation was also obtained through survey questionnaire, though the exact wording of the question(s) is not made clear. The analysis controls for the following nine case and defendant characteristics: the seriousness of the charge; whether the defendant was released on bail; the plea of the defendant; whether the defendant's counsel was privately retained; the defendant's sex; whether there

[17]Discriminant function analysis predicts group membership based on a linear combination of interval variables (Stockburger 2001).

[18]For example, there are currently at least 171 individual mandatory minimum provisions in the federal criminal statutes (United States Sentencing Commission 2009) and 25 states have adopted three–strikes laws (Murphy 2009).

were multiple cases against the defendant; the number of previous misdemeanor convictions; the number of previous felony convictions; and the age of the defendant.

Gibson (1978) finds little support for his initial hypothesis that liberals are more lenient sentencers. When he adds the judges' role orientations (conceptualized as the degree of ideological influence allowed) it appears that role orientation is intervening between ideology and sentence. The author explains, "[R]ole orientation specifies… the range of legitimate criteria of decision making… The data demonstrated that the role orientations of judges do indeed block the relationship between attitudes and behavior, a finding also consistent with the experimental literature" (1978, 922). But, as he goes on to note, "The generalizability of this model of decision making is indeed limited by the small number of judges analyzed [and] the lack of comparative data" (1978, 922). Moreover, one must wonder if the judges' self–reported ideology (one of the two main independent variables) is truly a non–biased indicator.[19]

Following the release of what could be considered his 'state of the theory' piece, Gibson (1981a) endeavors to avoid the pitfalls he observed as well as put a new conceptualization of role orientation to use. This research attempts to determine the effect of self–esteem on role orientation. Gibson (1981a) hypothesizes that the *role characteristics* of judges low in self esteem will be more strongly influenced by the *role expectations* of others than will the role characteristics of judges with high self esteem.[20] To determine if this is indeed the case, interviews were conducted in 1977 with 48 California judges who were selected because they shared a common trait—each had previously been elected to the legislature prior to becoming a judge. The judges' self–esteem was first gauged. Next, the judges' perceptions of role expectations were measured by asking the judges to rate nine *role alters* in terms of their importance in defining the 'proper' behavior for judges.[21]

Two indices were created from these responses. The first indicates the degree of importance ascribed to the expectations of external role alters (the media, the public, political party leaders, and attorneys), while the second indicates the importance of the expectations of internal role alters (trial judges, legal organizations, appellate judges, and attorneys). Judges were then asked to rate 19 stimuli on the degree of legitimate influence they should have on judicial decision–making. *Role behavior* was determined by asking the judges to indicate how often they overturn or

[19]Often, individuals have very different conceptualizations of what the term 'liberal' and 'conservative' mean. Therefore, when self–reporting ideology, these judges (like participants of other surveys) might very well have characterized themselves in ways that an objective party might not. This could be most pronounced in surveys of elites, where self–reporting a particular ideology might be in an individual's best interest.

[20]Briefly, *role characteristics* are the behaviors believed appropriate for a particular role occupant. *Role alters* are those who interact with the role occupant. Each role alter has *role expectations*, or normative beliefs, about how the role occupant ought to behave. For a more detailed discussion, see the section entitled "Conceptualizing the Judicial Role Orientation" below.

[21]The concept of role alters is very similar to a recently developed theory in the field of psychology of judicial decision–making. In *Judges and Their Audiences: A Perspective on Judicial Behavior*, Baum (2006) argues that judicial decision–making is influenced by judges' interest in popularity and respect. Moreover, Baum (2006) maintains that this regard for audience approval holds not just as a means to other ends, but also for that regard in–and–of itself.

significantly modify precedents in making decisions (1981a, 115).[22] Gibson's (1981a) results lend support to the idea that the impact of role expectations is strongly contingent upon the self–esteem of the judge.

There are two causes for concern with this work, however. First, because the judges are not selected at random, but rather because they share a common trait, the generalizability of these findings is unknown. It is certainly plausible to believe that individuals who have held both a legislative position *and* a judicial position are different from the general population of judges. This could be the case for several reasons—two of which go to the core of Gibson's (1981a) study. First, the experience of serving in the legislature could cause these judge–legislators to have a different role orientation than the typical judge. Second, the level of self–esteem required to subject oneself to a campaign for both a legislative position and judicial position might be significantly higher than the self–esteem required to only seek a judicial position, particularly during this time when judicial campaigns were less aggressive. Thus a study of the judge–legislators' self esteem is only applicable to other judge–legislators.

Second, the research lacks any data on the actual behavior of the judges. Asking how often a judge overturns or significantly modifies precedent creates a great probability of inaccuracy, either because the judge does not know this statistic or cannot accurately recall it when asked during an interview. In addition, the psychological theory of cognitive dissonance tells us that an individual wishing to minimize the discomfort of appearing inconsistent will only report behavior consistent with their self–identified role orientation.[23]

Following several years' void of judicial role orientation research, Scheb and Ungs's (1987) survey of 75 judges of the Tennessee court system reveals two role orientations: 'restraint–institutionalist' and 'activist–realist.' The authors do not find judicial role orientations to be either the rational choice of an autonomous actor or the determinant of the social, economic, and political environment. Rather, they suggest, the judicial culture supplies individuals with certain intellectual and behavioral parameters of permissibility and that individuals develop their particular role orientations within these parameters.

While creating an eleven–point scale for each question in order to allow judges variation in their responses is certainly an advancement, the authors do not take advantage of this available variation but rather dichotomize the role orientations. In addition, because all judges that operate under the state of Tennessee (except local judges) were surveyed and the results combined, any difference in role orientation among judges at the different court levels was ignored by the authors. Finally, Scheb and Ungs (1987, 398) acknowledge the uncertainty about the generalizability of their study: "We are confident that our survey results can be generalized to the population of Tennessee judges from which our sample is drawn. Whether these results apply to state court judges generally is unknown, and we make no such claim."

---

[22] *Role behavior* is the term used for role–relevant activity.

[23] For a seminal work on cognitive dissonance, see Festinger (1957). For a thorough examination of cognitive dissonance in the arena of judicial decision–making, see Collins (2011).

In the final study on the role orientation of state judges, Scheb et al. (1991) set out to empirically test Gibson's (1978) model.[24] In order to do so, 151 active state high court judges were surveyed. The judges were asked to identify their role orientation and ideology. This self–reported role orientation and ideology were then used to predict the judges' support for the prosecution in nonunanimous criminal cases. The authors find: (1) judicial role orientation is independent of ideology; (2) contrary to their expectation, role orientation and behavior are directly related; and (3) judicial 'activists' do not appear more ideological than their 'restraintist' colleagues.

This study suffers from several weaknesses. Most importantly, although high court judges from many states were surveyed, no institutional variables are included in the analysis. This is a significant fault because, in role theoretic terms, the institutional design of the court determines who some of the relevant role alters are.[25] Second, judges were asked to identify their own ideology. As noted above, survey respondents often have very different definitions for the terms 'liberal' and 'conservative.' Therefore, when self–reporting ideology, these judges, like any other individual, might very well characterize themselves in ways that an objective party might not.[26]

Despite the existence of a voluminous literature, substantial opportunity remains for scholarship on the judicial role orientation. First, as almost all of the existing scholarship on judicial role orientation examines trial court judges,[27] the existing literature does not adequately explore the role orientation of appellate judges, a group of individuals who, because of their place atop each state's judiciary, play an even more important role in our legal system. As role theory explains, one's role orientation is a synthesis of the role expectations of various role alters given one's environment. Therefore, because trial and appellate court judges operate in different environment and have some number of different role alters who possess different role expectations, it is reasonable to believe that the role orientation of each will be different. As such, attempts to leverage research on trial judges' role orientations to explain appellate judges' role orientations are less than optimal.[28]

Second, the existing research on appellate role orientation is not cross–institutional. A state's mechanism for the selection and retention of its judges provides constraints within which judges operate. These mechanisms are meant, by design,

---

[24] Behavior = Attitudes + Role Orientations + (Attitudes × Role Orientations).

[25] In states that popularly elect judges, for example, the voters are relevant role alters and, as such, their role expectations are legitimate decisional stimuli that must be given decisional weight by the judges of that state. Likewise, in states where the legislature selects members of the court, the legislators are relevant role alters and, therefore, their role expectations are legitimate decisional stimuli that must be given decisional weight by the judges of that state.

[26] For example, though measures of the ideology of Supreme Court justices developed by scholars place former–Justice John Paul Stevens as the Court's most liberal member (see, e.g., Martin and Quinn 2002), Justice Stevens couldn't disagree more. "I don't think of myself as a liberal at all. I think as part of my general politics, I'm pretty darn conservative" (Rosen 2007).

[27] See, e.g., Becker (1966), Gibson (1977, 1978, 1981b), and Jaros and Mendelsohn (1967).

[28] Likewise, combining trial and appellate court judges into a single analysis, as Gibson (1981a), Scheb and Ungs (1987), and Ungs and Baas (1972) do, in order to determine role orientation is also questionable because of the differences in environments, role alters, and role expectations.

to affect the decision–making process of the judges within that state by signaling to the judge who relevant role alters ought to be. States that make judges stand for popular election do so to provide incentive for judges to take the will of the people into account and provide the people with recourse (in the form of removal from office) against those judges who fail to do so (Bonneau and Hall 2009, 2–3). Legislative or executive appointments attempt to remove popular sanctions for unpopular rulings, thereby insulating judges from political pressure. States that use merit selection do so to reward attorneys and judges for doing what those on selection committees deem appropriate by granting said committees the power of judicial appointment. In a similar fashion, a long tenure is meant to insulate judges from frequent review (and potential removal from office) while a short tenure is meant to keep judges on a 'short leash.'

These institutional structures matter not because they force judges to rule in a particular manner, or even because they affect behavior directly, but rather because they signal to judges what stimuli can or should legitimately be allowed to influence decision–making. As Gibson (1978, 918) notes, "The basic function of decision–making role orientation is to specify what variables can legitimately be allowed to influence decision–making, and in the case of conflict, what priorities to assign to different decisional criteria."

Finally, much of the previous scholarship suffers from an inadequate conceptualization and/or operationalization of role orientation. Researchers often conceptualize role orientation as having a direct relationship to behavior. "For instance, a typical hypothesis is that 'activism' is related to 'liberal' decisions. Yet there is no theoretical structure supporting such a hypothesis—activism may be in favor of conservative values (e.g., the Hughes Court) or liberal values (e.g., the Warren Court)" (Gibson 1981b, 292).[29] Role theory should instead be conceptualized, as it is argued below, as a specification of what stimuli it is proper to allow to influence decision–making, and in the case of conflict, what priorities should be assigned to the different stimuli.

In addition, role orientation is almost always operationalized in such a way that there is little to no variation in the reported orientation. It is extremely unlikely that judges are as homogeneous as their responses to survey and interview questions have made them appear (Gibson 1981b, 296–297). If judges were that homogeneous it would make us question most of what we *know* about judges. Finally, few attempts have been made to demonstrate the impact of role orientation on the decision–making process. Those that have often use the judge's own reports of his or her behavior, such as how often he or she overturns precedent, rather than objectively observing role behavior.

[29]For more on this distinction, see the discussion below in the section entitled "Operationalizing the Judicial Role Orientation."

## 2.2 A Role Theoretic Framework

As perhaps two of the subject's most influential sociologists, Thomas and Biddle (1966, 4), write, "Individuals in society occupy positions, and their role performance in these positions is determined by social norms, demands, and rules; by the role performances of others in their respective positions; by those who observe and react to the performance; and by the individual's particular capabilities and personality." This, in short, describes role theory, a perspective that is said to have begun life as a theatrical metaphor,[30] yet, intellectually, can be traced to two theoretical trends in sociology: the symbolic interactionism of Cooley (1902), Mead (1934), and Blumer (1969)[31] and the structural–functionalism of Linton (1936), Parsons (1951), and Merton (1957).[32]

### 2.2.1 *Conceptualizing the Judicial Role Orientation*

The way individuals act within an institution differs from the way they act in non–institutional settings; that is to say, environment influences behavior. *Roles* are the constraints imposed on decision–makers by institutional structure. These roles limit, but do not eliminate, discretion in the interest of advancing organizational objectives (Gibson 1981b, 292–293). "[R]ole theory provides a means of moving beyond an exclusive focus on individuals to consider the influence of the institutional constraints on decision making" (Gibson 1983, 17) because "institutions exist... to circumscribe the alternatives available to the decision–maker" (Gibson 1981b, 293).

Roles do not constrain behavior alone, however. Role expectations are the normative beliefs held by the role occupant and role alters—or those who interact with

---

[30] Since performances in the theater are differentiated and predictable because actors are constrained to performing parts for which scripts are written, early scholars found it reasonable to believe social behaviors in other contexts could also be associated with parts and scripts understood by social actors (Biddle 1986, 68).

[31] As Knowles (1982, 6) describes, the symbolic interactionist perspective on roles developed in order to account for how an individual becomes a member of society. The essential answer provided by this school of thought is that the self does not exist without the social group because it is only through interaction with others that individuals learn to identify, label, and value objects.

[32] The structural–functionalist perspective, on the other hand, grew out of attempts to represent the social system. The basic assumption of this perspective is that "actions are patterned into coherent and ordered systems that govern both interpersonal interaction and societal functioning. Actions are patterned, in this sense, because certain aspects of behavior seem more characteristic of the relationship or the setting than of the particular individuals involved" (Knowles 1982, 6–7). Structural–functionalists assume that the social structure is known and that this knowledge is commonly shared. As Davis (1948, 88) described this assumption, an individual carries his role orientation around in his head, putting it into action when the appropriate occasion arises. He adds that, "[n]ot only does he carry it in his head but others also carry it in theirs, because [role orientations] are matters of reciprocal expectations and must be publicly and commonly conceived by everyone in the group."

the role occupant—about how the role occupant ought to behave. For example, it is expected that all judges are (at least somewhat) constrained by precedent. The extent to which this role expectation influences judicial decision–making varies, however, by the judge's position within the judiciary, the value the judge assigns precedent over other decisional criteria, the expectations of influential role alters, the age of the precedent, etc. "Each role occupant must synthesize these expectations, accepting some, rejecting others, to form a role orientation, a belief about proper behavior within the institutional position" (Gibson 1983, 17). Role–relevant activity is known as role behavior.

Thus, there is no consensually accepted judicial role orientation. Rather the process is "stochastic and is one of individuals' reacting in a variety of distinctive ways to the expectations they experience" (Gibson 1983, 17). Because the position of judge is incredibly complex, "judges' beliefs about the limits of proper behavior are also complex" (Gibson 1981b, 302). 'Proper' in this context does not refer to the policy content, but rather to the process of decision–making and, in particular, the kinds of stimuli that should influence decisions. "Some judges may believe it proper to be influenced by a particular stimulus while other judges may regard the stimulus as improper. More generally, judges vary in the breadth of stimuli they deem legitimate" (Gibson 1978, 918).

Following in the steps of Gibson, role orientation is conceptualized here as the stimuli, or variables, that a judge feels can legitimately be allowed to influence his or her decision–making and, in the case of conflict among influences, what priorities to assign to different decisional criteria. This conceptualization of role orientation is completely compatible with the norms for judging.

> A central expectation of judicial and legal traditions concerns the decision–making criteria employed by judges. For instance, equality before the law is not an empirical statement; it does not assert that individual litigants are in fact equal. Rather, the phrase is an exhortation to ignore the variables (stimuli), such as power, on which litigants are unequal and render decisions only on variables that provide for equality. For instance, it is generally regarded as illegitimate to discriminate on the basis of social class in sentencing decisions. This means that it is illegitimate to allow the social class of the defendant to influence the decision: class should be weighted at zero. Similarly, such concepts as the presumption of innocence in criminal cases are expectations that court officials will not allow empirical stimuli relating to the factual guilt of the defendant to influence their pretrial decisions (Gibson 1981b, 302-303).

### 2.2.2 *Operationalizing the Judicial Role Orientation*

While few terms describing a court or judge can conger a more visceral reaction, either positive or negative, the competing notions of judicial 'activism' and judicial 'restraint' provide an avenue for the operationalization of role orientation. In *Measuring Judicial Activism*, Lindquist and Cross (2009) note, the origin of the term judicial 'activism' can be traced to historian Arthur Schlesinger who, in an article on the U.S. Supreme Court, described 'activist' judges as those most inclined to use judicial power "for their own conception of the social good" and 'restraintist' judges as those most predisposed to "expand the range of allowable judgement for legislatures" (1947, 201). Though Schlesinger coined the term, the theoretical underpinnings of the debate around judicial 'activism' be traced back to the framing of the U.S. Constitution (Lindquist and Cross 2009, 2).[33]

In academic circles, the debate around judicial 'activism' has taken two tracks: one normative and the other empirical. Along the normative line, Thayer (1893), and his contemporaries, argue that a court (a counter–majoritarian body) should not overrule a legislature's (a majoritarian body) evaluation of their "legislation's wisdom and constitutionality" (Lindquist and Cross 2009, 21). This is true, according to Thayer et al., for both theoretical and practical reasons. Theoretically speaking, Bickel (1962, 27), for example, maintains, "democracies do live by the idea... that the majority has the ultimate power to displace the decision–makers and to reject any part of their policy." Moreover, "when the Supreme Court declares unconstitutional a legislative act or the action of an elected executive, it thwarts the will of representatives of the actual people of the here and now; it exercises control, not in behalf of the prevailing majority, but against it" (1962, 16–17).

Practically speaking, according to Tushnet (1999, 57–65), the presence of judicial 'activism,' or judicial supremacy, weakens the work of legislators in three important ways: it promotes irresponsibility, distorts legislation, and misleads legislators. Tushnet's (1999, 57–58) first criticism of judicial supremacy, adopted from Thayer (1893), postulates that legislators feel they need not concern themselves with the constitutionality of their work since courts will ultimately review the legislation and determine its legality. Second, judicial activism, according to Tushnet (1999, 60), distorts legislation because the possibility of a court striking down its work might cause the legislature to pursue laws that "could not accomplish what its members, and the American people want[]." Finally, the public nature of modern confirmation hearings incentivizes legislators to ask policy questions of nominees, yet, at the same time, incentivizes nominees to avoid answering such questions, to inadequately explain (either to the legislators or the public) constitutional law when they do, or, possibly, to distort their own jurisprudence (Tushnet 1999, 63–65).[34]

On the other side of the normative debate is Miller, and his contemporaries, who argue that result–oriented judges are good "because of the limits of the conventional electoral process. Insulated from this process, the judiciary could be a force for 'decency'..." (Lindquist and Cross 2009, 24). This is true, according to these scholars, for both theoretical and practical reasons. Theoretically speaking, Miller (1982) postulates, after considering the preamble to the Constitution, that justice should be a driving goal of the United States. Defining justice as "the satisfaction of basic human needs [that] can be summed up in the concept of human dignity" (1982, 168), courts should play two roles in securing justice:

[33]For an excellent discussion of the history of judicial 'activism,' as well as an examination of the extent to which U.S. Supreme Court justices engage in such activity, see Lindquist and Cross (2009).

[34]But, see, Collins and Ringhand (2013).

> First, accountability of those who exercise governing power, insofar as it is within the capacity of the High Bench to impose it, must encompass the affirmative dimension of justice as defined above. Second, ...[c]ourts as part of the political process cannot avoid deep and continuing involvement in the never–ending quest for social justice. However much judges have reflected, and still reflect, the wishes and values of the governing class in America, they and others in government must confront and deal with—effectively, one hopes—the growing passionate desires of people everywhere for both a fair shake of the social (and thus the legal) dice and a fair share of the planet's riches...Judges, including those on the the Supreme Court, can participate in society's struggles and labors: they can assist in making government officers (public and private) in the Corporate State accountable, both procedurally and substantively...[A]n avowed commitment to human dignity should be emblazoned on the escutcheons of those who serve on the nation's courts.

These arguments come not only from scholars, but also from judges themselves. For example, in his treatise on constitutional interpretation, *Active Liberty: Interpreting Our Democratic Constitution*, U.S. Supreme Court Justice Stephen Breyer (2005, 109–110) writes, "reference to the Constitution's basic democratic objectives can help courts shape constitutional doctrine, reconcile competing constitutional values, time judicial intervention, interpret statutory ambiguities, and create room for agency interpretations... I, a judge who has a role in playing the complex score provided me in the form of constitutional and statutory text, history, structure, and precedent, can perform my role with less discord, more faithfully to the entire enterprise, and with stronger justification for the power I wield in a government that is of, by, and for the people, by paying close attention to the Constitution's democratic active liberty objective."

Practically speaking, Peretti (1999, 100) argues that the selection system for the federal judiciary and the benches' frequent turnover ensures courts who are dynamically representative of the values currently dominant in the society and in the government. The judges' value–voting based decision–making, therefore, is a "democratic proxy of sorts" (1999, 132). "Contrary to the conventional view that it is arbitrary, idiosyncratic, and illegitimate," she argues, "value–voting may instead be regarded as a source of coherence, predictability, and democratic legitimacy" (1999, 132).

Providing a conservative defense of judicial supremacy, Bolick (2007, A.15) maintains, "[J]udicial activism—defined as courts holding the president, Congress, and state and local governments to their constitutional boundaries—is essential to protecting individual liberty and the rule of law... [and] was essential to the scheme of republican government established by our Constitution." Bolick concludes, "Properly wielded, a court gavel can be David's hammer against the Goliath of big government. Among our governmental institutions, courts alone are designed to protect the individual against the tyranny of the majority—and against special interest groups with outsized influence" (2007, A.15).[35]

Like the normative debate surrounding the legitimacy of judicial 'activism,' the academic debate surrounding its prevalence is likewise diverse. For example, in an early seminal work, Dahl (1957) finds that the U.S. Supreme Court upholds statutes enacted by the current national majority; only voting to strike those statutes enacted

[35] See, also, Barnett (1987).

by national majorities no longer in power. "The fact is, then, that the policy views dominant on the Court are never for long out of line with the policy views dominant among the lawmaking majorities of the United States. Consequently it would be most unrealistic to suppose that the Court would, for more than a few years at most, stand against any major alternatives sought by a lawmaking majority" (1957, 285).

In questioning Dahl's (1957) conclusions, Casper (1976, 50) writes, "Consideration of the way he interprets his own evidence and of other relevant evidence that is excluded from his analysis suggests that the Court participates more significantly in national policy making than Dahl's argument suggests." He continues:

> One reason that courts may have particular importance in placing issues on the agenda of other political institutions and in development of interest groups is that "success" in a court requires only that a party convince a relatively small number of decision makers. At the trial level, success requires only a favorable decision from a single individual; at the Supreme Court level, success requires the approval of five of nine. Thus, interests that lack resources for effective influence in legislative, executive, or administrative arenas may find the legal system an attractive spot in which to attempt to influence public policy. "Success" in a court then becomes useful in participation in these other arenas the court's decision may require other institutions to come to grips with an issue they have ignored; the legitimacy conferred by victory in court may be useful in attracting members and resources and mobilizing others (1976, 63).

Mishler and Sheehan (1993) find a U.S. Supreme Court much more responsive to public opinion than does Dahl (1957). Employing more sophisticated empirical testing than was available to either Dahl (1957) or Casper (1976), Mishler and Sheehan (1993, 96) conclude,

> For most of the period since 1956, a reciprocal relationship appears to have existed between the ideology of the public mood in the United States and the broad ideological tenor of Supreme Court decisions. The impact of the public mood on the Court's decisions occurs at a moderate lag; a somewhat shorter lag appears to exist in the reciprocal effects of Supreme Court decisions on public opinion. That both are strongly positive suggests the existence of a responsive Court whose decisions not only reflect changes in public opinion but also serve to reinforce and legitimize opinion change in an iterative process.

Following logically from the conceptualization of judicial role orientation adopted above, and grounded firmly in the judicial 'activism' literature, this study operationalizes judges' role orientations as being somewhere on a continuum that ranges from 'restraintist' to 'activist.' A 'restraintist' judge will be one who believes that precedent, the strict construction of constitutions, and giving deference to legislative intent are extremely important decisional criteria.[36] An 'activist' judge, on the other hand, will be one who gives greater decisional weight to personal attitudes, values, and case outcomes (Gibson 1983, 17–18).[37] This operationalization improves upon others in that it will allow for a direct examination of the degree to which role orientations influence judges' voting behavior.

---

[36]This term, at least loosely, corresponds to what some other role theoretic scholars term the 'law–interpreter,' 'institutionalist,' and 'interpreter' role orientation.

[37]Likewise, other scholars have referred to similarly defined role orientations as 'law–maker,' 'realist,' and 'innovator.'

A few final notes on this operationalization are necessary. First, despite what many commentators and politicians might assert, 'judicial activism' is not the same as liberalism, nor is 'judicial restraint' the same as conservatism.[38] Conceptually, as Itoh (2010, 263) writes, "The judicial role of activism and restraint is different from the judicial attitudes of liberalism and conservatism and should be kept separate for the purpose of judicial decision–making analysis." For his analysis, "The former refers to relations between the judiciary and the political branches and depicts the conflict and harmony between both sides whereas the latter describes judicial attitudes toward civil rights and liberties… There are conceptually four pairs of judicial behavior between the two variables" (2010, 263).

In the present analysis, given the operationalization of judges' role orientations as being 'activist' if greater decisional weight is given to personal attitudes, values, and case outcomes and 'restraint' if precedent, the strict construction of constitutions, and giving deference to legislative intent are instead given greater decisional weight, there are also four pairs of judicial behavior between the two variables: (1) A judge is an 'activist' if he or she would vote to strike down a law even if it is conservative; (2) A judge is an 'activist' if he or she would vote to strike down a law even if it is liberal; (3) A judge is a 'restraintist' if he or she would vote to uphold a law even if it is conservative; and (4) A judge is a 'restraintist' if he or she would vote to uphold a law even if it is liberal. These are each regardless of the judge's own ideology.

Recently, scholars have sought to make clear the distinction between the unrelated concepts of judicial roles, classified as 'activist' and 'restraintist,' and judicial attitudes, classified as liberalism and conservatism. For example, Howard and Segal (2002) systematically test the influence textual and originalism arguments have on the decisions of U.S. Supreme Court justices. To do so, the authors examine all merits briefs filed by petitioners and respondents in 1979, 1980, 1985, 1986, 1991, 1992, 1993, and 1994 looking for language indicating explicit textual support,[39] or implicit original intent support.[40] The authors find, "Anomalies aside, Justices might speak about following an 'originalist' jurisprudence, but they only appear to do so when arguments about text and intent coincide with the ideological position that they prefer" (2002, 133).

Similarly, Epstein and Landes (2012) test Judge Posner's (2012) suggestion that the common notion of judicial 'restraint,' a reluctance by judges to declare legislation or executive action unconstitutional out of deference to the judgments of the elected branches of government, is dead. To do so, the authors construct a dataset of U.S. Supreme Court cases that consider the constitutionality of federal laws between 1937–2009. Epstein and Landes (2012, 557) find that while "there was such a thing as judicial self–restraint, but there no longer is, just as Judge Posner suggests." Justices

[38]Indeed, the "inherently pejorative" connotation of the term 'judicial activism' has led some to call for the adoption of a more neutral "judicial engagement [which] doesn't call for a particular result. It calls for a particular approach to judging" (Neily, 2013).

[39]Such phrases include: 'plain meaning,' 'plain language,' or 'the language.'

[40]These include: references to legislative history and arguments about the original intent of the framers or the original meaning of the Constitution.

appointed since the 1960s are ideological in their approaches to the constitutionality of federal laws, such that "liberal justices are significantly more likely to strike conservative laws, and conservative justices are more likely to strike liberal laws" (2012, 567).

Likewise, Epstein and Martin (2012) question whether the Roberts Court is especially 'activist,' with 'activism' being defined as the propensity to strike down laws as unconstitutional. The authors conclude that the Roberts justices "just as their immediate predecessors, are neither uniform activists nor committed restraintists... In a nutshell, liberal Justices tend to invalidate conservative laws and conservative Justices, liberal laws. This holds regardless of whether we examine all the Justices' votes simultaneously or each Justice individually" (2012, 737–738).

Second, while the 'activist–restraintist' spectrum is an operationalization of the judicial role that makes logical sense and is firmly rooted in the literature, there are, of course, alternative dimensions of the judicial role orientation. For example, in his groundbreaking book, *Judges and Their Audiences: A Perspective on Judicial Behavior*, Baum (2006) theorizes that, rather than just considering the traditional attitudinal or legal influences on judicial decision–making, we should also consider that judges might as well be influenced by relevant audiences. Judges, Baum (2006, 4) argues, "care about the regard of salient audiences because they like that regard in itself, not just as a means to other ends."

This makes intuitive sense. As Baum (2006, 3) notes, people outside the academic world would have an easy time explaining some judicial behavior: "judges, like other people, get satisfaction from perceiving that other people view them positively." Yet scholars have been reluctant to entertain a notion so readily understandable by laymen. Why? Because it is extraordinarily difficult to empirically test this theory. First, as Baum (2006, 171–172) himself notes, a judge's relevant audiences must be identified. If dealing with a small number of judges, archival, interview, and survey data might be useful in these regards. But, such tools are of little use when dealing with many judges. Second, a dependent variable of judicial behavior that could be explained by the influence of an audience must be created.[41]

While this work does not directly operationalize a judge's role orientation in terms of following the will of salient audiences, its conceptualization of role orientation presumes such an influence is possible and its operationalization does allow for such an influence. Indeed, one strength of this role theoretic approach is that it allows for the inclusion of relevant audiences through the concepts of role alters and role expectations. As described above, an individual's role orientation is the product of his own expectations for proper role behavior, the expectations of various role alters (or audiences), and the constraints imposed by the institution within which he finds himself. Therefore, in the present analysis, it is assumed that a judge will consider the role expectations of role alters in regards to their 'activism.'

---

[41] For example, scholars typically operationalize judicial behavior as a judge's decision in a case. This is often in the form of a conservative or liberal vote. It is not obviously clear how an audience might affect that variable. Instead, a dependent variable that might be susceptible to a measurable audience effect would need to be adopted.

A similar, though not identical dimension, is one that considers judges' orientation toward the public they serve. This dimension of role orientation, included in Flango et al.'s (1975) analysis, identified mid–level appellate judges in Austria and Switzerland who ranged from not at all concerned with community to very concerned with community. Though the instant study does not include such an explicit dimension, just as discussed with Baum (2006) above, the conceptualization and operationalization adopted here does allow for such an influence. Moreover, one of the questions used in this study to measure the judges' role orientations at least measures a component of such a dimension.[42]

Another possible dimension of the role orientation is the court's agreement or disagreement with the political branches. Such an operationalization, as adopted by Itoh (2010), is not practical in the present study due to this study's scope. As the goal of this project is to survey the entire population of state high court judges (over 350 individuals) to obtain their role orientations, determine the causes of role orientation development, and test the effect role orientations have on judicial decision–making, a doctrinal case analysis approach such as Itoh's (2010) is not feasible. That being said, the 'activism—restraintist' operationalization adopted here does measure the judges' own perception of harmony with the political branches. A judge is identified as a 'restraintist' if he or she feels, among other things, that deference should be given to the political branches. This would equate with at least the judges' attempt to harmonize with the political branches.

## 2.3 Conclusion

This research is motivated by the absence of a theoretically grounded and empirically tested answer to the puzzle of why some judges are motivated by providing what they see as good law while other judges are motivated by providing what they see as good policy. To begin the process of crafting such an answer, this chapter surveyed role theoretic literature from across the social sciences and from within the discipline of political science. In particular, weaknesses in the existing literature on the role orientations of state judges were identified.

Then, adopting and building on the existent literature, a theoretical framework grounded in the role theoretic literature was identified. This framework provides that judges' role orientations are the product of their own preconceived notions about proper behavior and the expectations of relevant others, given the institution within which they find themselves. This role orientation then determines for the judge which

[42]Survey respondents were asked, among other questions, whether judges should be allowed great discretion in decision-making in order to ensure that their decisions are 'just.' Judges' responses to this question at least indirectly allow for some measure of the public's influence in the judge's role orientation through the concept of justice.

decisional criteria are proper and, in the case of conflict among influences, what priorities should be accorded each. This conceptualization was then operationalized as lying on a spectrum that ranges from 'restraintist' to 'activist,' a practice clearly in line with the judicial role orientation and judicial decision–making literatures.

## References


Andeweg, Rudy B. 1997. "Role Specialisation or Role Switching? Dutch MPs Between Electorate and Executive." *Journal of Legislative Studies* 3(1): 110–127.

Barnett, Randy. 1987. "Judicial Activism is Necessary." *Legal Times,* April 27.

Baum, Lawrence. 2006. *Judges and Their Audiences: A Perspective on Judicial Behavior.* Princeton: Princeton University Press.

Becker, Theodore L. 1965. *Political Behavioralism and Modern Jurisprudence: A Working Theory and Study in Judicial Decision-Making.* Chicago: Rand McNally.

Becker, Theodore L. 1966. "A Survey Study of Hawaiian Judges: The Effect on Decisions of Judicial Role Variations." *American Political Science Review* 60(3): 677–680.

Bickel, Alexander M. 1962. *The Least Dangerous Branch: The Supreme Court at the Bar of Politics.* Indianapolis: Bobbs-Merrill.

Biddle, Bruce J. 1986. "Recent Developments in Role Theory." *Annual Review of Sociology* 12: 67–92.

Blumer, Herbert. 1969. *Symbolic Interactionism: Perspective and Method.* Englewood Cliffs: Prentice-Hall.

Bolick, Clint. 2007. "A Cheer for Judicial Activism." *Wall Street Journal,* April 3, A.15.

Bonneau, Chris W., and Melinda Gann Hall. 2009. *In Defense of Judicial Elections.* New York: Routledge.

Braman, Eileen. 2009. *Law, Politics and Perception: How Policy Preferences Influence Legal Reasoning.* Charlottesville: University of Virginia Press.

Breyer, Stephen. 2005. *Active Liberty: Interpreting Our Democratic Constitution.* New York: Alfred A. Knopff.

Casper, Jonathan D. 1976. "The Supreme Court and National Policy Making." *American Political Science Review* 70(1): 50–63.

Collins, Jr., Paul M. 2011. "Cognitive Dissonance on the U.S. Supreme Court." *Political Research Quarterly* 64(2): 362–376.

Collins, Jr., Paul M., and Lori A. Ringhand. 2013. *Supreme Court Confirmation Hearings and Constitutional Change.* Cambridge: Cambridge University Press.

Cooley, Charles Horton. 1902. *Human Nature and the Social Order.* New York: Scribner's Sons.

Dahl, Robert A. 1957. "Decision-Making in a Democracy: The Supreme Court as National Policy Maker." *Journal of Public Law* 6: 279–295.

Davis, Kingsley. 1948. *Human Society.* New York: Macmillan.

Epstein, Lee, and Andrew D. Martin. 2012. "Is the Roberts Court Especially Activist? A Study of Invalidating (and Upholding) Federal, State, and Local Laws." *Emory Law Journal* 61: 737–758.

Epstein, Lee, and William M. Landes. 2012. "Was There Ever Such a Thing as Judicial Self-Restraint?" *California Law Review* 100(3): 557–578.

Festinger, Leon. 1957. *A Theory of Cognitive Dissonance.* Evanston: Row, Peterson.

Flango, Victor Eugene, Lettie McSpadden Wenner, and Manfred W. Wenner. 1975. "The Concept of Judicial Role: A Methodological Note." *American Journal of Political Science* 19(2): 277–289.

Friend, Hugo. 1954. "Appellate Judges Tell How Opinions Get That Way." *Illinois Bar Journal* 43: 156–158.

Gherghina, Sergiu. 2011. "MPs' Role Orientations in Newly Emerged Democratic Legislatures." *Journal of Legislative Studies* 17(1): 45–64.

Gibson, James L. 1977. "Discriminant Functions, Role Orientations and Judicial Behavior: Theoretical and Methodological Linkages." *Journal of Politics* 39(4): 984–1007.
Gibson, James L. 1978. "Judges' Role Orientations, Attitudes, and Decisions: An Interactive Model." *American Political Science Review* 72(3): 911–924.
Gibson, James L. 1981a. "Personality and Elite Political Behavior: The Influence of Self Esteem on Judicial Decision Making." *Journal of Politics* 43(1): 104–125.
Gibson, James L. 1981b. "The Role Concept in Judicial Research." *Law & Policy* 3(3): 291–311.
Gibson, James L. 1983. "From Simplicity to Complexity: The Development of Theory in the Study of Judicial Behavior." *Political Behavior* 5(1): 7–49.
Hadley, David J. 1977. "Legislative Role Orientations and Support for Party and Chief Executive in the Indiana House." *Legislative Studies Quarterly* 2(3): 309–335.
Howard, Jr., J. Woodford. 1977. "Role Perceptions and Behavior in Three U.S. Courts of Appeals." *Journal of Politics* 39(4): 916–938.
Howard, Robert M., and Jeffrey A. Segal. 2002. "An Original Look at Originalism." *Law & Society Review* 36(1): 113–138.
Itoh, Hiroshi. 2010. *The Supreme Court and Benign Elite Eemocracy in Japan*. Surrey: Ashgate.
James, Dorothy B. 1968. "Role Theory and the Supreme Court." *Journal of Politics* 30(1): 160–186.
Jaros, Dean, and Robert I. Mendelsohn. 1967. "The Judicial Role and Sentencing Behavior." *Midwest Journal of Political Science* 11(4): 471–488.
Kerlinger, Fred N. 1964. *Foundations of Behavioral Research: Educational and Psychological Inquiry*. New York: Holt, Rinhart and Winston.
King, Anthony. 1976. "Modes of Executive–Legislative Relations: Great Britain, France, and West Germany." *Legislative Studies Quarterly* 1(1): 11–36.
Knowles, Eric S. 1982. "From Individuals to Group Members: A Dialectic for the Social Sciences." In *Personality, Roles, and Social Behavior*, ed. William Ickes, and Eric S. Knowles. New York: Springer-Verlag.
Latham, Earl. 1952. *The Group Basis of Politics: A Study in Basing–Point Legislation*. Ithaca: Cornell University Press.
Lindquist, Stefanie A., and Frank B. Cross. 2009. *Measuring Judicial Activism*. Oxford: Oxford University Press.
Linton, Ralph. 1936. *The Study of Man: An Introduction*. New York: Appleton-Century-Crofts.
Martin, Andrew D., and Kevin Quinn. 2002. "Dynamic Ideal Point Estimation via Markov Chain Monte Carlo for the U.S. Supreme Court, 1953-1999." *Political Analysis* 10(2): 134–153.
Martin, John D. 1945. "After a Decade: The Reflections of a Trial and Appellate Judge." *American Bar Association Journal* 31: 625.
Mead, George H. 1934. *Mind, Self, and Society: From the Standpoint of a Social Behaviorist*. Chicago: University of Chicago Press.
Medina, Harold. 1963. "The Trial Judge's Notes: A Study in Judicial Administration." *Cornell Law Quarterly* 49(1): 1–11.
Merton, Robert K. 1957. *Social Theory and Social Structure: Toward the Codification of Theory and Research*. Glencoe: Free Press.
Miller, Arthur Selwyn. 1982. "In Defense of Judicial Activism." In *Supreme Court Activism and Restraint*, ed. Stephen C. Halpern, and Charles M. Lamb. Lexington: Lexington Books.
Mishler, William, and Reginald S. Sheehan. 1993. "The Supreme Court as a Countermajoritarian Institution?: The Impact of Public Opinion on Supreme Court Decisions." *American Political Science Review* 87(1): 87–101.
Murphy, Kim. 2009. "Washington State Revisits Three-Strikes Law." *Los Angeles Times,* August 11.
Neily, III, Clark M. 2013. *Terms of Engagement: How the Courts Should Enforce the Constitution's Promise of Limited Government*. New York: Encounter Books.
Parker, Sharon K. 2007. "'That Is My Job' How Employees' Role Orientation Affects Their Job Performance." *Human Relations* 60(3): 403–434.
Parsons, Talcott. 1951. *The Social System*. Glencoe: Free Press.

Peretti, Terri Jennings. 1999. *In Defense of a Political Court*. Princeton: Princeton University Press.
Posner, Richard A. 2012. "The Rise and Fall of Judicial Self–Restraint." *California Law Review* 100(3): 519–556.
Prewitt, Kenneth, Heinz Eulau, and Betty H. Zisk. 1966. "Political Socialization and Political Roles." *Public Opinion Quarterly* 30(4): 569–582.
Rosch, Teryl Ann, and Jill N. Reich. 1996. "The Enculturation of New Faculty in Higher Education: A Comparative Investigation of Three Academic Departments." *Research in Higher Education* 37(1): 115–131.
Rosen, Jeffrey. 2007. "The Dissenter." *The New York Times,* September 23.
Scandura, Terri A., and Belle Rose Ragins. 1993. "The Effects of Sex and Gender Role Orientation on Mentorship in Male-Dominated Occupations." *Journal of Vocational Behavior* 43(3): 251–265.
Scheb, II, John M., and Thomas D. Ungs. 1987. "Competing Orientations to the Judicial Role: The Case of Tennessee Judges." *Tennessee Law Review* 54(Spring): 391–411.
Scheb, II, John M., Terry Bowen, and Gary Anderson. 1991. "Ideology, Role Orientations, and Behavior in the State Courts of Last Resort." *American Politics Quarterly* 19(3): 324–335.
Schlesinger, Jr., Arthur M. 1947. "The Supreme Court: 1947." *Fortune,* January.
Segal, Jeffrey A., and Harold J. Spaeth. 1996. "The Influence of Stare Decisis on the Votes of United States Supreme Court Justices." *American Journal of Political Science* 40(4): 971–1003.
Shivers-Blackwell, Sheryl L. 2004. "Using Role Theory to Examine Determinants of Transformational and Transactional Leader Behavior." *Journal of Leadership and Organizational Studies* 10(3): 41–50.
Spence, Janet T. 1984. "Masculinity, Feminity, and Gender-Related Traits: A Conceptual Analysis and Critique of Current Research." *Progress in Experimental Personality Research* 13: 1–97.
Spence, Janet T., and Robert L. Helmreich. 1978. *Masculinity and Femininity: Their Psychological Dimensions, Correlates, and Antecedents*. Austin: University of Texas Press.
Stockburger, David W. 2001. *Multivariate Statistics: Concepts, Models, and Applications*. 2nd ed. http://www.psychstat.missouristate.edu/multibook2/mlt.htm (December 4, 2009).
Tarter, Ralph E., Donald I. Templer, and Rhoda L. Perley. 1975. "Social Role Orientation and Pathological Factors in Suicide Attempts of Varying Lethality." *Journal of Community Psychology* 3(3): 295–299.
Thayer, James Bradley. 1893. "The Origin and Scope of the American Doctrine of Constitutional Law." *Harvard Law Review* 7: 129–156.
Thomas, Edwin J., and Bruce J. Biddle. 1966. "The Nature and History of Role Theory." In *Role Theory: Concepts and Research*, ed. Bruce J. Biddle, and Edwin J. Thomas. New York: John Wiley & Sons.
Truman, David B. 1951. *The Governmental Process: Political Interests and Public Opinion*. New York: Alfred A. Knopf.
Tushnet, Mark. 1999. *Taking the Constitution Away from the Courts*. Princeton: Princeton University Press.
Ungs, Thomas D., and Larry R. Baas. 1972. "Judicial Role Perspectives: A Q-Technique Study of Ohio Judges." *Law & Society Review* 6(3): 343–366.
United States Sentencing Commission. 2009. *Overview of Statutory Mandatory Minimum Sentencing*. http://www.ussc.gov/manmin/man_min.pdf (December 4, 2009).
van Vonno, Cynthia M. C. 2012. "Role-Switching in the Dutch Parliament: Reinvigorating Role Theory?" *Journal of Legislative Studies* 18(2): 119–136.
Wahlke, John C., William Buchanan, Heinz Eulau, and LeRoy C. Ferguson. 1960. "American State Legislators' Role Orientations Toward Pressure Groups." *Journal of Politics* 22(2): 203–227.
Wold, John T. 1974. "Political Orientations, Social Backgrounds, and Role Perceptions of State Supreme Court Judges." *Western Political Quarterly* 27(2): 239–248.

# Chapter 3
# Insights from State High Court Judges

A substantial amount of data is needed to test the theory developed, conceptualized, and operationalized in Chap. 2. Given that it has been over 20 years since the last comprehensive investigation of the role orientations of state high court judges was undertaken, current data were needed. Though judges are a notoriously difficult population to survey, it is the only way to obtain all of the necessary data, so a nationwide mail survey to capture the role orientations, as well as relevant personal characteristics and professional experiences, of all state high court judges was crafted. This chapter begins, in Sect. 3.1, with a discussion of the survey design and implementation process that was developed. It concludes, in Sect. 3.2, with a discussion and exploration of the survey results.

## 3.1 The Survey Design

Several modes of survey were considered. As the goal was to investigate the high court judges from all 50 states, the resources (both in time and money) were not available to conduct in–person interviews. Phone interviews were deemed impractical from a time perspective (for both the principal investigator and the survey respondents). Internet surveys were considered, though ultimately rejected for the possible effects on both response rate and non–response bias.[1] Therefore, it was concluded that a

[1] The population of state high court judges is significantly older than the general population; the median age for survey respondents is 62 years–old compared to the median age for the general population of 37.2 years–old (Howden and Meyer 2011). Research reveals that, generally, as age increases, individuals are less likely to use the Internet and, in fact, only 48% of Americans over the age of 65 do so (Pew Internet & American Life Project 2012). With regard to the population of judges, while the use of technology in the courtroom has increased in recent years (Dixon 2011), e–mail is certainly used less frequently than postal mail by judges and would likely be viewed



R.V. Carman, Jr., *Making Good Law or Good Policy?*,
DOI 10.1007/978-3-319-53381-0_3

mail survey would be the most effective use of resources, garner the best response rate, and have the lowest potential for non–response bias.

Having chosen the survey mode that was believed would deliver the highest response rate with the lowest potential for error, the task of designing the mail survey began. Questions were carefully constructed to obtain the desired information while being clear, non–biased, professional, and technically correct. Closed–ended questions were used whenever possible to minimize any potential respondent confusion and provide for clear post–survey coding. Strategies provided by Dillman et al. (2009) for question and questionnaire design were employed whenever possible. The survey design and language was reviewed by faculty at five colleges, an analyst at the Administrative Office of the U.S. Courts, and a research associate at the Federal Judicial Center.[2] Suggestions from these individuals were incorporated wherever possible.

The survey questionnaire was printed on light blue, legal–sized (8.5 in. by 14 in.) paper. Two sheets of paper, with print appearing on both sides, were used for each questionnaire. As "questionnaires should be presented in conventional formats that people are used to handling…" and "… the most common format is a book or booklet with pages that are taller than they are wide…," (Dillman et al. 2009, 185) the questionnaire was prepared in a booklet format with double stapling in the spine. This presented a questionnaire booklet to the judges with a total of eight pages, each 8.5 in. by 7 in.

The front page of the questionnaire booklet, the entirety of which is reproduced in the Appendix, was the front cover, which included the title of the project, *Insights from State High Court Judges*,[3] an image of a gavel, and the following human subjects' notice: "This survey has been approved by the Binghamton University Human Subjects Research Review Committee (HSRRC). If you have any questions regarding your rights as a participant, contact the HSRRC at (607) 777–3818. Professor Wendy L. Martinek and Ph.D. Candidate Raymond V. Carman,

(Footnote 1 continued)
more skeptically. As such, it was believed that employing an Internet survey would produce a lower response rate and introduce both coverage error and nonresponse error.

[2]Comments were received from: Sara C. Benesh, Ph.D., Associate Professor, Department of Political Science, University of Wisconsin–Milwaukee; Jolly A. Emery, Ph.D. Associate Professor, Department of Political Science, University of Wisconsin–Whitewater; Lisa M. Holmes, Ph.D., Associate Professor, Department of Political Science, University of Vermont; Jennifer Jensen, Ph.D., Associate Dean for Academic Affairs, Harpur College of Arts and Sciences, Binghamton University; Wendy L. Martinek, Ph.D., Associate Professor, Department of Political Science, Binghamton University; Caroline L. Payne, Ph.D., Assistant Professor, Department of Political Science, Lycoming College; Kevin M. Scott, Ph.D., Social Science Analyst, Office of Judges Programs, Administrative Office of the U.S. Courts; Margaret S. Williams, Ph.D., Research Associate, Federal Judicial Center; and Jonathan Williamson, Ph.D., Assistant Professor, Department of Political Science, Lycoming College.

[3]Following the suggestions of Dillman et al. (2009, 192), the title *Insights from State High Court Judges* was chosen as it would "describe what [the] survey is about…," "have broad appeal to the respondents…," and not make the questionnaire "appeal to some types of respondents while being a turn–off to others." It also served to deemphasize the potentially controversial goal of measuring the role orientation of the judges.

Jr. are the principal investigators of this study. Professor Martinek can be reached at `martinek@binghamton.edu` or (607) 777–6748. Raymond Carman can be reached at `raymond.carman@binghamton.edu`."

The back page of the survey questionnaire booklet was the back cover, which thanked the judge for participating in the survey, provided a box for any comments or thoughts the judge had about the questionnaire, and displayed the logo of Binghamton University and the address of the Department of Political Science. It also contained the notice: "To receive survey results, please provide your name, address, and e–mail address on the enclosed sheet. This sheet will be separated from your survey to protect the anonymity of your answers." While it is customary, in order to increase response rates, to offer some form of monetary incentive,[4] offering a monetary incentive for judges who participated in the study would raise ethical questions, which would vary by state. Therefore, the non–monetary incentive of providing a summary of the survey results was offered to respondents who completed the questionnaire and mailed back an enclosed survey insert.

In addition, as "[e]ach questionnaire should have an individual identification number printed on it or printed on a label and affixed to it" (Dillman et al. 2009, 266), the lower left corner of the back cover contained a unique identification number that tracked the round of survey, the judge's state, and the individual judge.[5] The identification number was included "so that follow–up mailings, an essential aspect of tailored design, can be sent only to nonrespondents…" because "[r]emoving those who have already responded from the follow–up mailing list ensures that they are not inconvenienced, confused, or irritated by additional mailings that do not apply to them" (Dillman et al. 2009, 266).

The portion of the survey questionnaire that contained questions for the judges to answer was six booklet pages in length. Pages were numbered in the center of each page's footer. The survey questions fit broadly within three categories: the judge's professional experiences, the judge's current position, and the judge's demographic characteristics. Each category had its own labeled section and each fit onto two booklet pages. Each booklet page contained a single column of numbered questions, with numbering that started anew upon completion of each category (Dillman et al. 2009, 187). Key words within the questions were bolded for easy identification. Square checkboxes were used whenever possible for ease of both completing the questionnaire and coding the survey responses.

---

[4] Survey design research long ago found that "[o]ne of the largest contributors to improved response rates, second only to multiple contacts…, is the appropriate use of prepaid token financial incentives" (Dillman et al. 2009, 238). According to Dillman et al. (2009, 238), this token serves two purposes: (1) it brings social exchange into play thereby encouraging respondents to reciprocate by completing the survey; and (2) as it is a novel and unexpected gesture, it brings additional attention to the request so that respondents read and contemplate the survey rather than just throwing it away. For an examination of the effectiveness of various advance incentives, see Lesser et al. (2001).

[5] For example, the code "1–01–01" corresponds with the first wave of the survey, sent to the judge identified as "01" in the state coded as "01." Likewise, the code "2–05–05" corresponds with the second wave of the survey, sent to the judge identified as "05" in the state coded "05.".

During summer 2011, the entire population of high court judgeships from the 50 states was identified using state judiciary websites. Of the 349 judgeships identified, four seats were vacant at that time. A database with the contact information for the 345 judges to be surveyed was complied using information available from each state high court website. On August 3, 2011, the application material for expedited review was submitted to the Binghamton University Human Subjects Research Review Committee. As the data collection method was a survey questionnaire and the subjects of the survey project were elected or appointed public officials, the project was granted exempt approval on August 10, 2011.

Essential for maximizing the response rate to mail surveys, Dillman et al. (2009, 242–243) report, are multiple contacts that are different from previous ones. "[T]he later contacts need to be varied in an effort to increase their effectiveness with nonrespondents (who were not convinced to participate by tactics used in earlier requests)" (Dillman et al. 2009, 243). The authors suggest a system of five contacts: (1) a brief prenotice letter, (2) the survey questionnaire mailing, (3) a thank you postcard, (4) a replacement questionnaire, and (5) a final contact made by a different mode of delivery (Dillman et al. 2009, 243). The survey design implemented in this study adopted the first four contacts.[6]

As noted by Dillman et al. (2009, 244), studies have consistently demonstrated that sending a prenotice improves the response rates to mail surveys by 3 to 6% points (see, also, Dillman 1991; Dillman et al. 1995; Fox et al. 1988; Kanuk and Berenson 1975). The goal of the prenotice letter is to provide "a positive and timely notice that the recipient will be receiving a request to help with an important study or survey. It should be brief, personalized, positively worded, and aimed at engendering enthusiasm and building anticipation rather than providing the details or conditions for participation in the study" (Dillman et al. 2009, 244).

The prenotice letter for this study, the text of which is reproduced in the Appendix, was printed on Binghamton University Department of Political Science letterhead and contained contact information for the Binghamton University Human Subjects Research Review Committee and the principal investigators in order to convey a sense of legitimacy and increase the response rate by emphasizing university sponsorship (Dillman et al. 2009, 398). The letters were personalized, to the extent possible, by printing the judge's name and office address as the inside address, using the judge's name and title in the salutation, and individually signing each letter in blue ink.[7] In addition, the prenotice letter was mailed in a Binghamton University Department of Political Science envelope with the judge's name and office address printed on it and

[6]As Dillman et al. (2009, 243) explain, "[a]lthough this five–contact system has worked effectively in many studies, there is some room for modification." When returns from the fourth contact is very small, such as was the case in this project, the probable increase in returns from a fifth contact do not warrant the costs of an additional contact (Dillman et al. 2009, 243). In addition the survey project was designed with the conscious desire not to aggravate or alienate any of the judges, which adding a fifth contact might have done.

[7]A significant body of research has found that personalizing contacts, through the insertion of name and address, use of sponsor's stationery, and blue ink signatures, modestly increases response rates to mail surveys versus unpersonalized contacts (Dillman et al. 2007).

a first–class stamp affixed for postage (Dillman et al. 2009, 261). The prenotice letter was mailed to all 345 state high court judges on August 22, 2011.

One week later, on August 29, 2011, the first wave of the survey questionnaire was mailed. As Dillman et al. (2007, 246) note, sending only a questionnaire to potential respondents is "unlikely to result in very high response rates. Instead, the questionnaire mailing should contain a number of important pieces that contribute to the goals of reducing barriers and increasing motivation to respond." Therefore, included in the questionnaire mailing was a survey invitation cover letter, a survey insert, the questionnaire, and a postage–paid return envelope.

Written in a relatively brief and engaging way and conveying a sense of trustworthiness, the goals of the survey invitation cover letter are four–fold: (1) communicate to respondents what they are being asked to do, (2) inform why they are being asked to do it, (3) explain how they should go about doing it, and (4) identify what benefit will come from doing it (Dillman et al. 2007, 246). Like the prenotice letter, the survey invitation cover letter, the text of which is reproduced in the Appendix, was printed on Binghamton University Department of Political Science letterhead and contained contact information for the Binghamton University Human Subjects Research Review Committee and the principal investigators in order to convey a sense of legitimacy and increase the response rate by once again emphasizing university sponsorship (Dillman et al. 2009, 398). In order to achieve the four goals defined by Dillman et al. (2007, 246), the survey invitation cover letter reminded the judges of the prenotice letter they received the previous week alerting them of this survey project, it asked the judges to complete and return the included survey questionnaire so that a comprehensive examination of state high court judges' background and professional experiences could be undertaken, it offered a summary of survey responses to interested respondents, and ensured confidentiality and the reporting of only aggregated responses. The survey invitation cover letters were personalized in the same manner as the prenotice letter.

As noted above, including an incentive is an effective measure to increase response rate as it brings social exchange into play and is a novel and unexpected gesture. However, judicial ethics and state law makes the typical monetary incentive difficult if not impossible to include with a survey questionnaire to judges. Therefore, serving as a non–monetary incentive, a survey insert was included that gave respondents the opportunity to receive a summary of the survey results by providing their contact information. Part of the way the survey project was framed to the judges was to say that, despite the extremely important function that high courts serve, little is known, collectively, about the individuals who serve these courts. While the survey responses would be of interest to political scientists, the results would also be of interest to the judges themselves. Thus the judges could learn more about their colleagues by completing the questionnaire and including a completed survey insert, reproduced in the Appendix.

The survey questionnaire mailing also included a self–addressed, first–class stamped reply envelope. A first–class stamped envelope is included because, within the social exchange framework, it serves three functions: (1) it reduces the resource costs to the respondent by making return of the questionnaire as easy as possible,

(2) it encourages trust that the questionnaire is important,[8] and (3) sending a real stamp represents a goodwill gesture (Dillman et al. 2009, 249). Research indicates that using first–class stamped reply envelopes improves response rates by a few percentage points over using post–paid postage business reply envelopes (see, e.g., Armstrong and Lusk 1987; Dillman et al. 1995).

The assembly of the survey questionnaire mailings were prepared so that all enclosures came out of the envelope at once and the appealing aspects of each element were immediately visible (Dillman et al. 2009, 263). Specifically, a Z fold was used so that the bottom third of the survey invitation cover letter and survey insert were folded upward over the middle third, and the top third was folded backward, resulting in paper that formed a Z shape (Dillman et al. 2009, 264). The folded survey invitation cover letter and survey insert were then flipped so that the top third was visible (and the text of the letter was right side up), and the questionnaire was placed between the top and middle thirds so that they rested in the V formed by the fold (Dillman et al. 2009, 264). The package was then placed into the envelope so that when the letter was removed from the envelope, all of the other materials came with it (Dillman et al. 2009, 264).

One week later, on September 5, 2011, a thank you postcard was mailed to all of the judges. Reproduced in the Appendix, the purpose of the postcard was three–fold: (1) thank those judges who completed and returned the survey questionnaire, (2) ask those who had not yet completed and returned the questionnaire to do so, and (3) offer a replacement questionnaire if it had not been received or had been misplaced (Dillman et al. 2009, 250). The choice of a postcard format over a letter was deliberate in that it contrasts with the prenotice letter and survey invitation cover letter, "because new stimuli have greater effect than repeated stimuli" (Dillman et al. 2009, 250). The postcard included Binghamton University's logo, the Department of Political Science's return address, a first–class postcard stamp, and was personalized with the judges' name and office address.

On October 3, 2011, a second wave of the survey questionnaire package was mailed. This mailing contained the same materials as the first wave and was prepared in the same manner. The exact text of the survey invitation cover letter for this mailing is reproduced in the Appendix, however the letter, printed on Binghamton University Department of Political Science letterhead, reminded the judges of the survey project, thanked those who had already completed and returned the questionnaire, urged those who had not yet completed and returned the questionnaire to do so, emphasized the importance of the survey project, offered a summary of survey results to interested respondents, ensured confidentiality and the reporting of only aggregated responses, and provided contact information for the Binghamton University Human Subjects Research Review Committee and the principal investigators. The tone of this letter was the strongest of all contacts, in that it communicated to the judges that they are receiving individual attention and reinforced messages contained in the three previous contacts that their responses are important to the success of the survey

[8]As Dillman et al. (2009, 249) offer, "Why else would this person have sent a stamped envelope that I can use for something else?".

project (Dillman et al. 2009, 255). The survey invitation cover letter for this mailing was personalized in the same manner as all other mailings.

The timing of each contact followed the suggestions of Dillman et al. (2009). The prenotice letter was given enough time to arrive and be processed before the survey questionnaire arrives, but the questionnaire was mailed before the judge would forget the prenotice (Dillman et al. 2009, 259). Likewise, the postcard was sent to arrive after the original request, but before the questionnaire had been discarded or lost (Dillman et al. 2009, 259). The second wave of questionnaire mailing was sent four weeks after the postcard mailing, so that responses had dwindled thereby considerably lowering the chance that respondents would receive another one (Dillman et al. 2009, 259).

## 3.2 The Survey Results

In total, 134 survey questionnaires were returned completed. Given the nature of the individuals being surveyed,[9] this provided a respectable response rate of 38.8%.[10] Not all respondents answered all questions, so the response rate for individual analyses vary. Particularly left incomplete were the first two pages of the questionnaire booklet, which given that they posed the least controversial questions (those about the respondents' professional backgrounds) and that 11 respondents in all failed to complete both pages, it is believed that the pages were stuck together and the respondents were unaware that they had missed two questionnaire pages. Also more likely to be left blank (probably intentionally in these cases) were the questions about party identification (10 respondents provided no answer), religiousness, and one or more of the questions intended to capture the respondents' role orientation.

Ideally, to test for non–response bias, survey respondents would be compared to the entire population on a variable–by–variable basis. Unfortunately, there is little readily available public data about most of what was asked on the survey questionnaire. Two variables that can be compared are gender and race,[11] so the percentages of

[9]Illustrating some of the challenges that arise when surveying judges, individual notes were received from the chief justices of two states. One chief justice, without reason, respectfully declined to participate in the study. The other stated that a "number of the questions on the survey instrument request information that would not be appropriate" to provide and, as such, neither the chief justice nor any of the other justices from that state would be completing the survey questionnaire.

[10]A sample of studies that relied upon mail surveys of state court judges reveal a response rate ranging from 26% for a random sample of state judges identified from published lists and almanacs (Stier et al. 1992) and a survey of all California Superior Court judges (Reidy et al. 1989), to 40% for all New York trial court judges (Jensen and Martinek 2009), and as high as 46% for a sample of Texas judges (Williams 2006).

[11]The partisan makeup of survey respondents versus the population of state high court judges was also explored. Since the only state high court judges for whom we have relatively reliable partisanship information are those that hold office in states that require these judges to stand for partisan election, the partisanship of the population of high court judges in those states was compared to the survey respondents from those states. In states that hold partisan elections for state high court judges, 61.3% of the judges were elected as Republicans. The partisan makeup of survey respondents

**Table 3.1** Gender and racial diversity of the population of state high court judges and survey respondents by U.S. Census Bureau Geographic Region

| Region | Female judges | | | Non-white judges | | |
|---|---|---|---|---|---|---|
| | Population (%) | Respondents (%) | Difference (%) | Population (%) | Respondents (%) | Difference (%) |
| Northeast | 33.3 | 34.8 | +1.5 | 10.5 | 4.3 | −6.2 |
| Midwest | 33.3 | 37.5 | +4.2 | 6.4 | 8.7 | +2.3 |
| South | 33.3 | 30.8 | −2.6 | 18.5 | 14.0 | −4.5 |
| West | 32.9 | 44.1 | +11.2 | 15.2 | 14.7 | −0.5 |
| Nationwide | 33.2 | 36.1 | +2.9 | 13.8 | 11.5 | −2.3 |

*Source* American Judicature Society (2010) and survey responses
*Note* Figures represent the percentage of the population of state high court judges within the geographic region who were identified as a female or minority by the American Judicature Society, the percentage of all survey respondents within the geographic region who indicated their gender or race on their survey response, and the difference between the population and survey respondents. A positive number indicates a response rate higher than the population, while a negative number indicates a response rate lower than the population

women and minority survey respondents were compared to the population of women and minority state high court judges using the most recently available data (American Judicature Society 2010).[12] Results, both by U.S. Census Bureau geographic region and nationwide, are presented in Table 3.1. Individual regional differences vary from a lower–than–expected response rate of 0.5% for minority judges in the Western region to a higher–than–expected response rate of 11.2% for female judges in the West. Nationwide, the response rate for female judges is 2.9% more than expected and the response rate for minority judges is 2.3% less than expected. This variation is not substantively large; therefore, it is believed that the survey respondents are a reasonable representation of the larger population.

Table 3.2 presents the background characteristics of survey respondents. Though results could be displayed in a number of ways, it was determined that providing survey responses by judicial selection method would provide both a venue for discussing the results as well as exploring the extent to which institutional context affects the composition of state judiciaries. As the nuances of each state's selection method differs greatly, the categorization adopted here is simplified yet still follows standard convention. A state is labeled partisan if the ballot on which the state's high court judges are selected lists the judges' partisan identification, nonpartisan if the ballot on which the state's high court judges are selected does not list the judges' partisan identification, merit if a nominating commission begins the judicial

(Footnote 11 continued)
from those states was 72.0% Republican. Thus Republicans responded by 10.7% more than expected in partisan election states.

[12]The gender and racial makeup of the population of state high court judges was compiled by the American Judicature Society during 2009 and 2010. The names and addresses for this study were compiled during summer 2011. Therefore, it is possible that any one court might have become either more diverse or less diverse in the time from the compilation of diversity figures by the American Judicature Society and the mailing of the survey questionnaires.

**Table 3.2** Background characteristics of survey respondents by judicial selection method

| Survey question | Partisan N = 18 | Nonpartisan N = 51 | Merit N = 52 | Legislature N = 5 | Gubernatorial N = 8 | All N = 134 |
|---|---|---|---|---|---|---|
| Basic demographics | | | | | | |
| Age | 61.8 | 60.9 | 61.0 | 62.0 | 64.1 | 61.3 |
| Gender (% Male) | 66.7% | 68.0% | 63.5% | 80.0% | 25.0%** | 63.9% |
| Education | | | | | | |
| Ph.D. | 0.0% | 0.0% | 2.0% | 0.0% | 0.8% | 0.8% |
| LL.M. | 11.1% | 4.1% | 11.8% | 20.0% | 0.0% | 8.4% |
| M.P.A. or M.P.P. | 5.6% | 0.0% | 0.0% | 0.0% | 12.5%*** | 1.5% |
| Other M.A. or M.S. | 11.1% | 16.3% | 9.8% | 20.0% | 0.0% | 12.2% |
| Ethnicity/Race[a] | | | | | | |
| African American/Black | 5.6% | 4.2% | 9.8% | 20.0% | 0.0% | 6.9% |
| Asian or Pacific Islander | 0.0% | 0.0% | 3.9% | 0.0% | 25.0%*** | 3.1% |
| Caucasian/White | 94.4% | 93.8% | 84.3% | 80.0% | 75.0% | 88.5% |
| Hispanic/Latino | 0.0% | 2.1% | 2.0% | 0.0% | 0.0% | 1.5% |
| Marital status | | | | | | |
| Divorced | 11.1% | 8.2% | 5.9% | 0.0% | 0.0% | 6.9% |
| Married/Partnered | 88.9% | 87.8% | 86.3% | 100.0% | 87.5% | 87.8% |
| Never married | 0.0% | 4.1% | 5.9% | 0.0% | 12.5% | 4.6% |
| Widowed | 0.0% | 0.0% | 2.0% | 0.0% | 0.0% | 0.8% |
| Partisanship[b] | | | | | | |
| Democrat | 22.2% | 41.3% | 47.9% | 50.0% | 50.0% | 41.9% |
| Republican | 72.2%*** | 19.6%** | 27.1% | 25.0% | 25.0% | 30.7% |
| Unaffiliated | 5.6%** | 37.0%** | 25.0% | 0.0% | 25.0% | 25.8% |
| Religion[c] | | | | | | |
| Catholic | 11.1% | 27.1%** | 7.8%** | 20.0% | 37.5% | 17.7% |
| Jewish | 0.0% | 4.2% | 9.8% | 0.0% | 12.5% | 6.2% |
| Protestant | 66.7% | 47.9% | 58.8% | 60.0% | 12.5%** | 53.1% |
| Born again | 38.5%* | 23.5% | 15.6% | 25.0% | 0.0% | 21.4% |
| None/Atheist/Agnostic | 22.2% | 12.5% | 21.6% | 0.0% | 37.5% | 18.5% |
| Religiousness | | | | | | |
| Every week | 33.3% | 25.5% | 16.3% | 50.0% | 12.5% | 23.0% |
| Almost every week | 5.6% | 14.9% | 16.3% | 25.0% | 12.5% | 14.3% |
| Once or twice a month | 5.6% | 12.8% | 12.2% | 25.0% | 12.5% | 11.9% |
| A few times a year | 27.8% | 25.5% | 30.6% | 0.0% | 37.5% | 27.8% |
| Never | 27.8% | 19.2% | 24.5% | 0.0% | 25.0% | 22.2% |

(continued)

Table 3.2 (continued)

| Survey question | Partisan N = 18 | Nonpartisan N = 51 | Merit N = 52 | Legislature N = 5 | Gubernatorial N = 8 | All N = 134 |
|---|---|---|---|---|---|---|
| Upbringing | | | | | | |
| Rural | 33.3% | 44.9%** | 27.5% | 0.0% | 32.8% | 32.8% |
| Suburban | 55.6% | 40.8% | 49.0% | 60.0% | 62.5% | 48.1% |
| Urban | 11.1% | 14.3% | 23.5% | 40.0% | 25.0% | 19.1% |

*Note* As selection methods vary greatly, the categorization reported here is partisan if the final ballot judges appear on lists the judges' party, nonpartisan if the final ballot judges appear on does not list the judges' party, merit if a nominating commission begins the selection process, legislative if the legislature begins selection process, and gubernatorial if the governor begins the selection process. Age is the mean age of survey respondents within each category. Other figures represent the percentage of survey respondents within each category who answered the survey question and signified that they identified with or possessed that particular characteristic. Column Ns represent the total number of survey respondents within each category. The number of respondents per survey question varies because not all survey respondents answered all questions. Significance levels reported reflect Pearson $\chi^2$ values. $*p < 0.1$, $**p < 0.05$, $***p < 0.01$

[a]No respondents identify as "Native American or Alaskan Native" or "Other"

[b]Any survey response that indicates the respondent feels they are independent or nonpartisan is coded as Unaffiliated

[c]Respondents were also given the response choice of "Other." Some responses include: buddhist, humanist, and "golden rule"

selection process, legislative if the legislature elects the judge, and gubernatorial if the governor begins the judicial selection process.

When asked, all but 11 respondents provided their current age. Ages were located via state court biographies and newspaper articles for 10 of these respondents who did not report their age. Survey respondents range from 37 years old to 80 years old. The mean age is 61.3, the median age is 62, and the modal age is 64. Given that these individuals are at the pinnacle of their career, it is unsurprising that the median age of the survey respondents is higher than 49, the median age for all lawyers in the United States (American Bar Association 2012). Age varies little by selection method. The selection method with the highest mean age is gubernatorial appointment (64.1), while the selection method with the lowest mean age is nonpartisan election (60.9).

Survey respondents were next asked to report with which gender they identify. All but four respondents responded to this question. For three of these four, the respondents' gender was obtained via state court biographies. As a majority of the population of state high court judges are male,[13] not surprisingly a clear majority (63.9%) of survey respondents are male. Interestingly, though, respondents who were appointed by their governor are significantly more likely to be female.[14] There is some basis in the literature to expect this finding. For example, Henry (1985) and

[13]See, American Judicature Society (2010).

[14]To determine if there is a statistically significant relationship between the variables of interest, tests of significance appearing in the rest of this chapter were achieved by calculating Pearson $\chi^2$ values. Results are only reported as significant if they report a probability of 0.10 or less that there is a relationship between the variables of interest.

Holmes and Emrey (2006) found that women are more likely to be appointed to state judiciaries by an executive than through either partisan or nonpartisan election. Likewise, Esterling and Andersen (1999) found that women are more likely to be appointed than elected (but see, Alozie 1996; Hurwitz and Lanier 2008).

It is important to note that, while well below what might be expected based upon the gender makeup of the entire U.S. adult population,[15] 36.1% of state high court judges being female is higher than the percentage of female lawyers in the United States,[16] and historically an all–time high. In 1980–1981, for example, Glick and Emmert (1986) found that only 3.1% of all state high court judges were female. While there is obviously still much improvement to be made before there exists gender equality on state high courts, women have made great strides towards that goal.

State high court judges were asked to indicate each advanced academic degree they have earned. The response options were: J.D., LL.M., Ph.D., M.P.A. or M.P.P., other M.A. or M.S., other, and none. All but three survey respondents answered this question. All respondents possess a J.D. This is a drastic change from 1961–1968, when only 57.4% of state high court judges had a Bachelors Degree (Canon 1972) and from 1980–1981 when only 80% had a Bachelors Degree (Glick and Emmert 1986). In addition, a total of 30 other graduate degrees have been earned by respondents. The most often held other advanced academic degree is an M.A. or M.S. Respondents appointed by their governor are significantly more likely to hold an M.P.A. or M.P.P.

Survey respondents were then asked, "What racial/ethnic group(s) best describe you (check all that apply)?" The response options were: "African American/Black," "Asian or Pacific Islander," "Caucasian/White, not of Hispanic/Latino origin," "Hispanic/Latino," "Native American or Alaskan Native," and "Other." All but four survey respondents answered this question. As in the population of state high court judges,[17] an overwhelming majority (88.5%) of respondents identify as White. Survey respondents who were appointed by their governor are significantly more likely to identify as Asian or Pacific Islander. Again, there is some basis in the literature for such a finding. For example, Henry (1985) and Holmes and Emrey (2006) found that minorities are more likely to be appointed to state judiciaries by an executive than are to ascend to the bench through either partisan or nonpartisan election. Likewise, Esterling and Andersen (1999) found that minorities are more likely to be appointed than elected (but see, Alozie 1996; Hurwitz and Lanier 2008).

While well below what might be expected based upon the racial makeup of the entire U.S. adult population,[18] 11.5% of state high court judges being a member of a minority group is consistent with the statistic for the population of lawyers in the United States (11.9%),[19] and historically an all–time high. In 1980–1981, for

---

[15]The U.S.Census Bureau (2014) reports that 50.8% of the U.S. population is female.

[16]The American Bar Association (2012) reports that 30% of lawyers are female.

[17]See, American Judicature Society (2010).

[18]The U.S.Census Bureau (2014) reports that 62.6% of the U.S. population is "White alone, not Hispanic or Latino.".

[19]See, American Bar Association (2012).

example, Glick and Emmert (1986) found that only 0.6% of all state high court judges were minorities. While there is obviously still much improvement to be made before there exists racial equality on state high courts, minorities have made great strides in addressing the inequality.

State high court judges were next asked about their current marital status. Survey respondents overwhelmingly identify as "Married/Partnered." Nationwide, 87.8% identify as married, or partnered, 6.9% identify as divorced, 4.6% identify as never married, and 0.8% identify as widowed. There is no statistically significant relationship between respondents' marital status and selection method.

To capture partisanship, state high court judges were asked a slightly modified version of the American National Election Studies (2012) partisanship question. Judges were asked, "Generally speaking, do you consider yourself a Democrat, a Republican, or something else?" To try to gently persuade survey respondents to supply a party identification (something it was believed judges might be reluctant to report), the response choices did not include an option for independent or unaffiliated but rather were limited to Democrat, Republican, and Other. However, any handwritten survey response that indicated that the respondent felt that they were independent or nonpartisan was coded as Unaffiliated.

In all, 124 out of 134 survey respondents answered this question. Nationwide, 41.9% of respondents identify as Democrat, 30.7% as Republican, and 25.8% as Unaffiliated. This is a drastic change from 1961–1968, when 57.4% of state high court judges were Democrats (Canon 1972) and from 1980–1981 when 67.0% were Democrats (Glick and Emmert 1986). Judges who are elected on a partisan ballot are more likely to be Republican and less likely (as might be expected) to be Unaffiliated. Judges who are elected on a nonpartisan ballot are more likely to be Unaffiliated and less likely to be Republican. There are no statistically significant effects for Democrats.

State high court judges were then asked, "Which of the following best describes your religious belief?" The response options were: "Catholic," "Jewish," "Protestant," "None/atheist/agnostic," and "Other." All but four survey respondents answered this question. A majority of survey respondents (53.1%) identify as Protestant. This is a drastic change from 1961–1968, when 80.3% of state high court judges were Protestant (Canon 1972) and a change from 1980–1981 when 60.2% were Protestant (Glick and Emmert 1986). Respondents elected on a partisan ballot are significantly more likely to report being born again and respondents elected on a nonpartisan ballot are significantly more likely to be Catholic. Respondents subject to merit selection are less likely to be Catholic and respondents who were appointed by their governor are significantly less likely to be Protestant.

To gauge how religious state high court judges are, they were asked, "Apart from weddings and funerals, how often do you attend religious services?" The response choices were: every day, almost every day, every week, almost every week, once or twice a month, a few times a year, and never. One hundred and twenty–six out of 134 survey respondents answered this question. Few survey respondents (0.8%) attend church every day, none attend church almost every day, though the most report attending services every week (23%) or almost every week (14.3%). Nearly one–third of survey respondents (27.8%) report attending church a few times a year and over 22% never attend services. There is no statistically significant relationship between religiousness and selection method.

Finally, survey respondents were asked, "How would you describe the area in which you spent or mostly spent your childhood?" In order to capture the type of environment in which the judge was brought up, it was deemed inaccurate to ask the more common question of where the respondent was born. Response options presented were, "Rural," "Suburban," and "Urban." Defining these response options by providing population ranges was considered, but ultimately not implemented as it was feared that few survey respondents would know the population of their childhood hometown at the time they lived there. A plurality of survey respondents (48.1%) indicate that they spent their childhoods in suburban environments. The next most common childhood environ is rural (32.8%). The fewest number of survey respondents (19.1%) were raised in urban areas. Respondents subjected to a nonpartisan ballot are significantly more likely to have been born in a rural setting.

The second section of the questionnaire asked state high court judges to indicate the type of law offices in which they had worked, the lower courts (if any) on which they had served, whether they had held an appointed or elected non–judicial office, and whether they were currently or had previously taught in a variety of educational settings. Nationwide, the most frequently reported (54%) legal experience was working in a small private practice (defined as those employing between 2 and 10 attorneys), while the least frequent (3%) was serving as in–house counsel.[20] Nearly 49% of respondents served as a state trial court judge before joining the state high court. Prior political experience of the respondents range from 5% having served in appointed federal office, to 30% having non–judicial elected experience. In terms of teaching experience, the greatest number of survey respondents teach or have taught law school (30%), while the fewest number of respondents teach or have taught in a graduate program (3%). Tables 3.3, 3.4, and 3.5 report professional experiences by gender, minority status, and judicial selection system, respectively.

By gender, the only statistically significant difference in legal experience is having served as in–house counsel — female survey respondents are significantly more likely to have served in that capacity. There is no significant variation by gender in prior judicial experience. In terms of political experience, males are significantly more likely to have held an appointed federal position and a non–judicial elected position. As to teaching experience, the only significant difference by gender is that males are more likely to teach or have taught at a four–year college or university.

Like gender, there are few differences in the professional experiences of minority and non–minority survey respondents. Minority survey respondents are, by a statistically significant margin, more likely to have worked in a large private practice (defined as those employing more than 51 attorneys) and non–minority survey

---

[20]These statistics are somewhat surprising given the figures reported by the American Bar Association (2012). In 2005, 1% of lawyers worked in a public defender's office, 8% worked for the government, 8% worked for private industry, and 75% worked in private practice. Of those in private practice, 49% of lawyers were sole practitioners, 20% worked in a small law firm, 12% worked in a medium law firm, and 20% worked at a large law firm.

**Table 3.3** Professional experiences of survey respondents by gender

| Survey question | Female judges N = 48 | Male judges N = 85 | All N = 133 |
|---|---|---|---|
| Legal experience | | | |
| Attorney general's office | 21.4% | 21.8% | 21.7% |
| District attorney's office | 26.2% | 30.8% | 29.2% |
| In–house counsel | 7.1%* | 1.3% | 3.4% |
| Practice, solo | 23.8% | 23.1% | 23.3% |
| Practice, small[a] | 45.2% | 59.0% | 54.2% |
| Practice, medium[b] | 21.4% | 19.2% | 20.0% |
| Practice, large[c] | 19.1% | 19.2% | 19.2% |
| Public defender's office | 4.8% | 7.7% | 6.7% |
| Public interest firm | 7.1% | 7.7% | 7.5% |
| Judicial experience | | | |
| Local trial | 17.8% | 14.6% | 15.8% |
| State trial | 53.3% | 46.3% | 48.8% |
| State intermediate app. | 37.8% | 29.3% | 32.3% |
| Political experience | | | |
| Appointed state | 20.9% | 34.2% | 29.5% |
| Appointed federal | 0.0% | 7.7%* | 5.0% |
| Elected | 18.6% | 36.7%** | 30.3% |
| Teaching experience | | | |
| Community college | 2.3% | 6.3% | 4.9% |
| Four–year college | 4.7% | 16.5%* | 12.3% |
| Law school | 32.6% | 29.1% | 30.3% |
| Graduate program[d] | 2.3% | 2.5% | 2.5% |

*Note* Figures represent the percentage of all survey respondents who indicated their gender, answered the survey question, and signified that they had previously worked in that particular position. Column Ns represent the total number of survey respondents by self–identified gender. The number of respondents per survey question varies because not all survey respondents answered all questions and not all survey respondents identified their gender. Significance levels reported reflect Pearson $\chi^2$ values. $*p < 0.1$, $**p < 0.05$, $***p < 0.01$

[a] A small firm was designated as those employing between 2 and 10 attorneys

[b] A medium firm was designated as those employing between 11 and 50 attorneys

[c] A large firm was designated as those employing 51 or more attorneys

[d] The examples of doctoral and masters programs were included next to the survey item 'Graduate program'

respondents are significantly more likely to have worked in a small private practice (defined as those employing between 2 and 10 attorneys). However, there is no significant difference in the judicial, political, or teaching experiences of minority and non–minority respondents.

However, as Table 3.5 reveals, there are more statistically significant differences in the professional experiences of survey respondents when examined by judicial selection method. Respondents subject to partisan election are significantly less likely

**Table 3.4** Professional experiences of survey respondents by minority status

| Survey question | Minority judges N = 13 | Non-minority judges N = 106 | All N = 130 |
|---|---|---|---|
| Legal experience | | | |
| Attorney general's office | 30.8% | 20.8% | 21.9% |
| District attorney's office | 30.8% | 29.3% | 29.4% |
| In–house counsel | 7.7% | 2.9% | 3.4% |
| Practice, solo | 15.4% | 24.5% | 23.5% |
| Practice, small[a] | 30.8% | 57.6%* | 54.6% |
| Practice, medium[b] | 15.4% | 20.8% | 20.2% |
| Practice, large[c] | 38.5%** | 16.0% | 18.5% |
| Public defender's office | 7.7% | 6.6% | 6.7% |
| Public interest firm | 0.0% | 8.5% | 7.6% |
| Judicial experience | | | |
| Local trial | 7.1% | 16.4% | 15.3% |
| State trial | 57.1% | 47.3% | 48.4% |
| State intermediate app. | 42.9% | 30.9% | 32.3% |
| Political experience | | | |
| Appointed state | 21.4% | 30.8% | 29.8% |
| Appointed federal | 7.1% | 4.7% | 5.0% |
| Elected | 21.4% | 31.8% | 30.6% |
| Teaching experience | | | |
| Community college | 0.0% | 5.6% | 5.0% |
| Four–year college | 14.3% | 12.2% | 12.4% |
| Law school | 21.4% | 30.8% | 29.8% |
| Graduate program[d] | 0.0% | 2.8% | 2.5% |

*Note* Judges are categorized as Non–Minority if their indicated race or ethnicity was Caucasian/White and Minority otherwise. Figures represent the percentage of all survey respondents who indicated their race and thus could be categorized, answered the survey question, and signified that they had previously worked in that particular position. Column Ns represent the total number of survey respondents categorized by self–identified race. The number of respondents per survey question varies because not all survey respondents answered all questions and not all survey respondents identified their race. Significance levels reported reflect Pearson $\chi^2$ values. *$p < 0.1$, **$p < 0.05$, ***$p < 0.01$

[a] A small firm was designated as those employing between 2 and 10 attorneys

[b] A medium firm was designated as those employing between 11 and 50 attorneys

[c] A large firm was designated as those employing 51 or more attorneys

[d] The examples of doctoral and masters programs were included next to the survey item 'Graduate program'

**Table 3.5** Professional experiences of survey respondents by judicial selection method

| Survey question | Partisan N = 18 | Nonpartisan N = 51 | Merit N = 52 | Legislature N = 5 | Gubernatorial N = 8 | All N = 134 |
|---|---|---|---|---|---|---|
| Legal experience | | | | | | |
| Attorney general's office | 26.7% | 21.3% | 21.3% | 20.0% | 16.7% | 21.7% |
| District attorney's office | 46.7% | 29.8% | 17.0%** | 20.0% | 83.3%*** | 29.2% |
| In–house counsel | 6.7% | 2.2% | 4.3% | 0.0% | 0.0% | 3.4% |
| Practice, solo | 6.7%* | 34.0%** | 19.2% | 20.0% | 16.7% | 23.3% |
| Practice, small[a] | 66.7% | 66.0%** | 38.3% | 60.0% | 50.0% | 54.2% |
| Practice, medium[b] | 6.7% | 17.0% | 25.5% | 40.0% | 16.7% | 20.0% |
| Practice, large[c] | 6.7% | 17.0% | 25.5% | 20.0% | 16.7% | 19.2% |
| Public defender's office | 0.0% | 10.6% | 4.3% | 20.0% | 0.0% | 6.7% |
| Public interest firm | 13.3% | 6.4% | 6.4% | 0.0% | 16.7% | 7.5% |
| Judicial experience | | | | | | |
| Local trial | 6.7% | 26.5%*** | 5.9%*** | 40.0% | 14.3% | 15.8% |
| State trial | 40.0% | 36.7%** | 56.9% | 60.0% | 85.7%** | 48.8% |
| State intermediate app. | 33.3% | 32.7% | 25.5% | 40.0% | 71.4%** | 32.3% |
| Political experience | | | | | | |
| Appointed state | 13.3% | 25.5% | 35.4% | 40.0% | 42.9% | 29.5% |
| Appointed federal | 6.7% | 4.3% | 6.3% | 0.0% | 0.0% | 5.0% |
| Elected | 33.3% | 36.2% | 20.8%* | 60.0% | 28.6% | 30.3% |
| Teaching experience | | | | | | |
| Community college | 0.0% | 10.6%** | 0.0%** | 20.0% | 0.0% | 4.9% |
| Four–year college | 6.7% | 12.8% | 12.5% | 20.0% | 14.3% | 12.3% |

(continued)

**Table 3.5** (continued)

| Survey question | Partisan N = 18 | Nonpartisan N = 51 | Merit N = 52 | Legislature N = 5 | Gubernatorial N = 8 | All N = 134 |
|---|---|---|---|---|---|---|
| Law school | 26.7% | 19.2%** | 39.6%* | 40.0% | 42.9% | 30.3% |
| Graduate program[d] | 0.0% | 2.1% | 4.2% | 0.0% | 0.0% | 2.5% |

*Note* As selection methods vary greatly, the categorization reported here is partisan if the final ballot judges appear on lists the judges' party, nonpartisan if the final ballot judges appear on does not list the judges' party, merit if a nominating commission begins the selection process, legislature if the legislature begins selection process, and gubernatorial if the governor begins the selection process. Figures represent the percentage of survey respondents within each category who answered the survey question and signified that they had previously worked in that particular position. Column Ns represent the total number of survey respondents within each category. The number of respondents per survey question varies because not all survey respondents answered all questions. Significance levels reported reflect Pearson $\chi^2$ values. $*p < 0.1$, $**p < 0.05$, $***p < 0.01$

[a]A small firm was designated as those employing between 2 and 10 attorneys

[b]A medium firm was designated as those employing between 11 and 50 attorneys

[c]A large firm was designated as those employing 51 or more attorneys

[d]The examples of doctoral and masters programs were included next to the survey item 'Graduate program'

to have worked as a sole practitioner, while respondents subject to a nonpartisan election are significantly more likely to have worked as a sole practitioner and in a small private practice (defined as those employing between 2 and 10 attorneys). Respondents selected by a merit–based system are significantly less likely to have worked in the district attorney's office, while respondents selected by their governor are significantly more likely to have worked in the district attorney's office. Survey respondents who were subject to a nonpartisan election are significantly more likely to have served on a local trial court and significantly less likely to have served on a state trial court. Respondents subject to merit selection are significantly less likely to have served on a local trial court. Respondents subject to gubernatorial appointment are significantly more likely to have state trial court experience and state intermediate court experience. Respondents subject to merit selection are significantly less likely to have been elected to a non–judicial position. Survey respondents who were selected in a nonpartisan election are significantly more likely to have taught or currently be teaching at a community college and are significantly less likely to have taught or currently be teaching at a law school. Finally, respondents selected through merit selection are significantly more likely to have taught or currently be teaching at a law school and significantly less likely to have taught or currently be teaching at a community college.

## 3.3 Conclusion

Despite the difficult nature of surveying judges, through careful design and implementation, the *Insights from State High Court Judges* survey received a very respectable 38.8% response rate. Overall, these survey results present an interesting portrait of state high court judges. While still not as diverse as the entire U.S. population, survey respondents represent a bench that is much more diverse now than it was in the 1960s and the 1980s in terms of gender, race, and partisan identification. The mean age of survey respondents is 61.3. While the typical respondent is a married, White Protestant male from a suburban locale, certain judicial selection methods lend themselves to statistically significant variations. For example, Asian or Pacific Islander respondents were more likely to be appointed by a governor and Protestant survey respondents were less likely to be appointed by a governor. Respondents subjected to nonpartisan ballot are significantly more likely to have been raised in a rural setting.

In terms of professional experience, a majority of survey respondents have worked in a small private practice, nearly half have served on a state trial court, nearly one–third have been elected to a non–judicial office, and nearly one–third are currently teaching or have taught at a law school. While there is little significance in the variation of the professional experiences of survey respondents when examined by gender and minority status, judicial selection method was correlated with differences in some professional experiences.

## Appendix

In this chapter, the survey design and implementation process, the results of which provide the bulk of data for this work, is chronicled. Receiving an acceptable response rate in a survey of judges is a notoriously difficult and time–consuming task. Materials must be carefully crafted to obtain the desired information while being clear, non–biased, professional, and technically correct. Reproduced in Appendix are the prenotice letter, survey invitation cover letter, survey instrument, survey insert, thank you postcard, and the second wave of survey mailing's survey invitation cover letter. I hope that future researchers find this survey material useful in designing their own survey.

## Prenotice Letter

August 22, 2011

The Honorable <First Name> <Middle Name> <Last Name>
<Court Name>
<Address>
<City>, <State> <Zip>

Dear <Title> <Last Name>:

As scholars who study the American judiciary, we know the vital role that state courts play in our nations legal system. Atop each states legal system sits a court of last resort that, for nearly all cases, provides the final legal word. Despite this extremely important function, little is known, collectively, about the individuals who serve their state as high court judges.

We are writing to ask for your help with an important study being conducted by the State High Court Project at Binghamton University to understand the background and professional experiences of state high court judges. In the next week you will receive a request to participate in this project by completing a short survey that is the core of this study. The survey takes only 5–10 min to complete, and return postage is paid.

We believe that this study is important not only to political scientists, but also to judges themselves, and we will provide a summary of project results to all interested respondents. We take great care to protect your privacy. All responses are confidential and survey results will only be reported in the aggregate.

If you have any questions regarding your rights as a participant, contact the Binghamton University Human Subjects Research Review Committee at (607) 777–3818. Professor Wendy L. Martinek and Ph.D. Candidate Raymond V. Carman, Jr. are the principal investigators of this study. Professor Martinek can be reached at `martinek@binghamton.edu` or (607) 777–6748. Raymond Carman can be reached at `raymond.carman@binghamton.edu`.

We hope you will consider participating in this important study.

Sincerely,

Raymond V. Carman, Jr.
Ph.D. Candidate

## Survey Invitation Cover Letter: First Mailing

August 29, 2011

The Honorable <First Name> <Middle Name> <Last Name>
<Court Name>
<Address>
<City>, <State> <Zip>

Dear <Title> <Last Name>:

Last week, we sent a letter to you about a study the State High Court Project at Binghamton University is conducting concerning the background and professional experiences of state court of last resort judges. We are now sending you the actual survey that is at the heart of this study. Would you please consider taking a few minutes to complete this brief survey? We believe that this study is important not only to political scientists, but also to judges themselves, and we will provide a summary of project results to all interested respondents.

You can return the survey, which has been approved by the Binghamton University Human Subjects Research Review Committee, in the enclosed postage–paid envelope. Please know that we take great care to protect your privacy. All responses are confidential and survey results will only be reported in the aggregate; under no circumstances will personally identifiable information be published or released. Your voluntary completion of the survey constitutes consent to participate.

If you have any questions regarding your rights as a participant, contact the Binghamton University Human Subjects Research Review Committee at (607) 777–3818. Professor Wendy L. Martinek and Ph.D. Candidate Raymond V. Carman, Jr. are the principal investigators of this study. Professor Martinek can be reached at `martinek@binghamton.edu` or (607) 777–6748. Raymond Carman can be reached at `raymond.carman@binghamton.edu`.

Thank you so much for your participation!

Sincerely,

Raymond V. Carman, Jr.
Ph.D. Candidate

## Survey Instrument

# INSIGHTS FROM STATE HIGH COURT JUDGES

This survey has been approved by the Binghamton University Human Subjects Research Review Committee (HSRRC). If you have any questions regarding your rights as a participant, contact the HSRRC at (607) 777-3818. Professor Wendy L. Martinek and Ph.D. Candidate Raymond V. Carman, Jr. are the principal investigators of this study. Professor Martinek can be reached at martinek@binghamton.edu or (607) 777-6748. Raymond Carman can be reached at raymond.carman@binghamton.edu.

**Professional Experiences:**

1. Please indicate **EACH** type of judge for which you have **CLERKED** (check all that apply):

   ❑ Federal trial ❑ State trial ❑ Local trial

   ❑ Federal appellate ❑ State appellate ❑ None

2. Please indicate the total number of **YEARS**, if any, that you have worked for a **GOVERNMENT** in each of the following settings:

| | Federal Gov't | State Gov't | Local Gov't |
|---|---|---|---|
| As a lawyer | ____ | ____ | ____ |
| As a judge | ____ | ____ | ____ |
| In another government position | ____ | ____ | ____ |

3. Please indicate the total number of **YEARS**, if any, that you have worked as an **ATTORNEY** in the following settings:

| | |
|---|---|
| Attorney General's office | ________ |
| District Attorney's office | ________ |
| In-house counsel | ________ |
| Private practice, 2 to 10 lawyers | ________ |
| Private practice, 11 to 50 lawyers | ________ |
| Private practice, 51 or more lawyers | ________ |
| Public Defender's office | ________ |
| Public interest firm or interest group | ________ |
| Solo practice | ________ |

4. Did you hold any **JUDGESHIPS PRIOR** to your **CURRENT** position?

   ❑ Yes ❑ No

   If so, what judgeship(s) did you hold?

   ______________________________________________

1

5. Have you ever held a **NON-JUDICIAL**, **APPOINTED** position in your **STATE** government?

❑ Yes ❑ No

If so, what non-judicial, appointed state position(s) did you hold?

___

6. Have you ever held a **NON-JUDICIAL**, **APPOINTED** position in the **FEDERAL** government?

❑ Yes ❑ No

If so, what non-judicial, appointed federal position(s) did you hold?

___

7. Have you ever run for an **ELECTED**, **NON-JUDICIAL** office?

❑ Yes ❑ No

If so, what elected, non-judicial office(s) did you run for?

___

8. Have you ever **TAUGHT** as a **FULL-TIME** or **ADJUNCT** instructor of law (not, for example, an occasional guest lecture in a class)?

❑ Yes ❑ No

If so, at what type of school(s) did you teach law (check all that apply)?

❑ Community college

❑ Four-year college or university

❑ Law school

❑ Graduate program (Ph.D., M.A., etc.)

2

**Current Position:**

1. Are you **CURRENTLY** serving your **FIRST** term on a state court of last resort?

   ❑ Yes ❑ No

   If you are **NOT** currently serving your **FIRST** term, how **MANY** terms had you completed prior to the start of your current term?

   __________

2. Were you **APPOINTED or ELECTED** to your **FIRST** term as a state court of last resort judge?

   ❑ Appointed to a full term

   ❑ Appointed to a fill an interim term

   ❑ Elected

3. If you competed in a nonpartisan or partisan **ELECTION** to secure your **CURRENT** term, did you face a **PRIMARY** opponent?

   ❑ Yes ❑ No

   If you faced a primary opponent, please indicate the **PERCENTAGE** of the vote that you received:

   __________

4. If you competed in a nonpartisan or partisan **ELECTION** to secure your **CURRENT** term, did you face a **GENERAL ELECTION** opponent?

   ❑ Yes ❑ No

   If you faced a general election opponent, please indicate the **PERCENTAGE** of the vote that you received:

   __________

3

5. Did you compete in a **RETENTION ELECTION** to secure your **CURRENT** term?

❑ Yes ❑ No

If you competed in a retention election to secure your current term, please indicate the **PERCENTAGE** of the vote that you received:

__________

6. Please indicate your level of **AGREEMENT** with **EACH** of the following six statements:

| | Strongly Disagree | Disagree | Agree | Strongly Agree |
|---|---|---|---|---|
| A good judge is one who sticks as closely as possible to precedents. | ❑ | ❑ | ❑ | ❑ |
| Judges should be allowed great discretion in decision-making in order to ensure that their decisions are "just." | ❑ | ❑ | ❑ | ❑ |
| It is wrong for a judge to allow his or her personal philosophy to influence his or her decisions. | ❑ | ❑ | ❑ | ❑ |
| Precedents are rarely conclusive; usually a judge can find a precedent that supports his or her own point of view. | ❑ | ❑ | ❑ | ❑ |
| Precedents and statutes are the main factors that should influence judges' decisions. | ❑ | ❑ | ❑ | ❑ |
| It is just as legitimate to make a decision and then find the precedent as it is to find the precedent and then make the decision. | ❑ | ❑ | ❑ | ❑ |

4

**Demographic Characteristics:**

1. Please indicate **EACH** advanced academic degree that you have earned (check all that apply):

   ❑ J.D. ❑ LL.M. ❑ Ph.D.

   ❑ M.P.A. or M.P.P. ❑ Other M.A. or M.S. ❑ None

   ❑ Other (Please specify: ____________________)

2. How would you describe the area in which you spent or mostly spent your childhood?

   ❑ Rural ❑ Suburban ❑ Urban

3. What is your age?

   __________

4. What is your gender?

   ❑ Female ❑ Male

5. What is your current marital status?

   ❑ Divorced ❑ Married/Partnered

   ❑ Never married ❑ Widowed

6. Do you have children?

   ❑ Yes ❑ No

7. What racial/ethnic group(s) best describes you (check all that apply)?

   ❑ African American/Black

   ❑ Asian or Pacific Islander

   ❑ Caucasian/White, not of Hispanic/Latino origin

   ❑ Hispanic/Latino

   ❑ Native American or Alaskan Native

   ❑ Other (Please specify: ____________________)

5

8. Generally speaking, do you consider yourself a Democrat, a Republican, or something else?
   - ❑ Democrat
   - ❑ Republican
   - ❑ Other (Please specify: ____________________)

9. Which of the following best describes your religious belief?
   - ❑ Catholic
   - ❑ Jewish
   - ❑ Protestant
   - ❑ None/atheist/agnostic
   - ❑ Other (Please specify: ____________________)

10. If you identify as a Christian, do you consider yourself born again?
    - ❑ Yes ❑ No

11. Apart from weddings and funerals, how often do you attend religious services?
    - ❑ Every day
    - ❑ Almost every day
    - ❑ Every week
    - ❑ Almost every week
    - ❑ Once or twice a month
    - ❑ A few times a year
    - ❑ Never

6

**Thank you for taking the time to complete this survey. Your participation is greatly appreciated!**

If you have any comments or thoughts about the survey, please share them here:

To receive survey results, please provide your name, address, and e-mail address on the enclosed sheet. This sheet will be separated from your survey to protect the anonymity of your answers. Using the enclosed postage-paid envelope, please return this sheet and your completed survey to:

State High Court Project
Department of Political Science
Binghamton University
Post Office Box 6000
Binghamton, NY 13902

BINGHAMTON
UNIVERSITY
STATE UNIVERSITY OF NEW YORK

1-FIPS-Judge #

## Survey Insert

### INSIGHTS FROM STATE HIGH COURT JUDGES

To receive a summary of survey results, please provide your name, address, and e-mail address below. This sheet will be separated from your survey to protect the anonymity of your answers. Using the enclosed postage-paid envelope, please return this sheet and your completed survey to:

State High Court Project
Department of Political Science
Binghamton University
Post Office Box 6000
Binghamton, NY 13902

NAME:

ADDRESS:

E-MAIL ADDRESS:

## Thank You Postcard

BINGHAMTON
UNIVERSITY
STATE UNIVERSITY OF NEW YORK

Department of Political Science
PO Box 6000
Binghamton, New York 13902 -6000

The Honorable <First_Name> <Middle_Name> <Last_Name>
<Court_Name>
<Address_1>
<City>, <State> <Zip>

September 5, 2011

Last week, a brief questionnaire was mailed to you by the State High Court Project at Binghamton University, which is conducting a study concerning the background and professional experiences of state court of last resort judges.

If you have already completed and returned the survey, please accept our sincere thanks. If not, would you please consider taking a few minutes to complete this very short survey? It will take less than 10 minutes of your time. We believe that this study is important not only to political scientists, but also to judges themselves, and we will provide a summary of project results to all interested respondents.

If you did not receive a questionnaire, or if it was misplaced, please call us at (607) 699-1415 and we will get another one in the mail for you today.

We are especially grateful for your help with this important study

Sincerely,

Raymond V. Carman, Jr., Ph.D. Candidate

## Survey Invitation Cover Letter: Second Mailing

October 3, 2011
The Honorable <First Name> <Middle Name> <Last Name>
<Court Name>
<Address>
<City>, <State> <Zip>

Dear <Title> <Last Name>:

Last month, we sent a survey to you that is the heart of a study the State High Court Project at Binghamton University is conducting concerning the background and professional experiences of state court of last resort judges. If you have already completed and returned the survey, please accept our sincere thanks. If not, would you please consider taking a few moments to complete this survey? It will take less than 10 min of your time. We believe that this study is important not only to political scientists, but also to judges themselves, and we will provide a summary of project results to all interested respondents.

You can return the survey, which has been approved by the Binghamton University Human Subjects Research Review Committee, in the enclosed postage–paid envelope. Please know that we take great care to protect your privacy. All responses are confidential and survey results will only be reported in the aggregate; under no circumstances will personally identifiable information be published or released. Your voluntary completion of the survey constitutes consent to participate.

If you have any questions regarding your rights as a participant, contact the Binghamton University Human Subjects Research Review Committee at (607) 777–3818. Professor Wendy L. Martinek and Ph.D. Candidate Raymond V. Carman, Jr. are the principal investigators of this study. Professor Martinek can be reached at `martinek@binghamton.edu` or (607) 777–6748. Raymond Carman can be reached at `raymond.carman@binghamton.edu`.

Thank you so much for your participation!

Sincerely,

Raymond V. Carman, Jr.
Ph.D. Candidate

## References


Alozie, Nicholas O. 1996. "Selection Methods and the Recruitment of Women to State Courts of Last Resort." *Social Science Quarterly* 77(1): 110–126.

American Bar Association. 2012. "Diversity of the Bench." http://www.americanbar.org/content/dam/aba/migrated/marketresearch/PublicDocuments/lawyer_demographics_2012_revised.authcheckdam.pdf (November 11, 2014).

American Judicature Society. 2010. "Diversity of the Bench." http://www.judicialselection.us/judicial_selection/bench_diversity/index.cfm (June 6, 2012).

American National Election Studies. 2012. "ANES 2008 Time Series Study." February 17. http://www.electionstudies.org/studypages/2008prepost/2008prepost.htm (June 5, 2012).

Armstrong, J. Scott, and Edward J. Lusk. 1987. "Return Postage in Mail Surveys: A Meta-Analysis." *Public Opinion Quarterly* 51(2): 233–248.

Canon, Bradley. 1972. "The Impact of Formal Selection Process on the Characteristics of Judges – Reconsidered." *Law & Society Review* 6: 579–593.

Dillman, Don A. 1991. "The Design and Administration of Mail Surveys." *Annual Review of Sociology* 17: 225–249.

Dillman, Don A., Jolene D. Smyth, and Leah Melani Christian. 2009. *Internet, Mail, and Mixed-Mode Surveys: The Tailored Design Method*. 3rd ed. Hoboken: John Wiley & Sons.

Dillman, Don A., Jon R. Clark, and Michael A. Sinclair. 1995. "How Prenotice Letters, Stamped Return Envelopes, and Reminder Postcards Affect Mailback Response Rates for Census Questionnaires." *Survey Methodology* 21(2): 159–166.

Dillman, Don A., Virginia Lesser, Robert Mason, John Carlson, Fern Willits, Rob Robertson, and Bryan Burke. 2007. "Personalization of Mail Surveys for General Public and Populations with a Group Identity: Results from Nine Studies." *Rural Sociology* 72(4): 632–646.

Dixon, Jr., Herbert B. 2011. "The Evolution of a High-Technology Courtroom." http://www.ncsc.org/sitecore/content/microsites/future-trends/home/Technology/1-4-Evolution-of-high-tech-courtroom.aspx (May 8, 2012).

Esterling, Kevin M., and Seth S. Andersen. 1999. "Diversity and the Judicial Merit Selection Process: A Statistical Report." In *Research on Judicial Selection*. Vol. 2. Chicago: American Judicial Society, 2–39.

Fox, Richard J., Melvin R. Crask, and Jonghoon Kim. 1988. "Mail Survey Response Rate: A Meta-Analysis of Selected Techniques for Inducing Response." *Public Opinion Quarterly* 52(4): 467–491.

Glick, Henry R., and Craig F. Emmert. 1986. "Stability and Change: Characteristics of State Supreme Court Judges." *Judicature* 70(2): 107–112.

Henry, M. L. 1985. *The Success of Women and Minorities in Achieving Judicial Office: The Selection Process*. New York: Fund for Modern Courts.

Holmes, Lisa M., and Jolly A. Emrey. 2006. "Court Diversification: Staffing the State Courts of Last Resort Through Interim Appointments." *Justice System Journal* 27(1): 1–13.

Howden, Lindsay M., and Julie A. Meyer. 2011. "2010 Census Briefs: Age and Sex Composition." May 26. http://www.census.gov/prod/cen2010/briefs/c2010br-03.pdf (May 8, 2012).

Hurwitz, Mark S., and Drew Noble Lanier. 2008. "Diversity in State and Federal Appellate Courts: Change and Continuity Across 20 Years." *Justice System Journal* 29(1): 47–70.

Jensen, Jennifer M., and Wendy L. Martinek. 2009. "The Effects of Race and Gender on the Judicial Ambitions of State Trial Court Judges." *Political Research Quarterly* 62(2): 379–392.

Kanuk, Leslie, and Conrad Berenson. 1975. "Mail Surveys and Response Rates: A Literature Review." *Journal of Marketing Research* 12(4): 440–453.

Lesser, Virginia M., Don A. Dillman, John Carlson, Frederick Lorenz, Robert Mason, and Fern Willits. 2001. "Quantifying The Influence of Incentives on Mail Survey Response Rates and Nonresponse Bias." Presented at the Annual Meeting of the American Statistical Association, Atlanta.

Pew Internet & American Life Project. 2012. "Demographics of Internet Users." February. http://www.pewinternet.org/Static-Pages/Trend-Data/Whos-Online.aspx (May 8, 2012).
Reidy, Thomas J., Richard M. Silver, and Alan Carlson. 1989. "Child Custody Decisions: A Survey of Judges." *Family Law Quarterly* 23(1): 75–87.
Stier, Max, Kelly M. Klaus, Dan L. Bagatell, and Jeffrey J. Rachlinski. 1992. "Law Review Usage and Suggestions for Improvement: A Survey of Attorneys, Professors, and Judges." *Stanford Law Review* 44(6): 1467–1513.
U.S. Census Bureau. 2014. "USA Quick Facts." July 8. http://quickfacts.census.gov/qfd/states/00000.html (July 21, 2014).
Williams, Margaret S. 2006. "The Process of Becomming a Judge for Women and Men." *Judicature* 90(3): 104–113.

# Chapter 4
# The Development of the Judicial Role Orientation

In arguing against the proposition that judicial decision–making is merely governed by "political considerations," Indiana Court of Appeals Judge Nancy Vaidik discusses the complexities of judicial discretion. While Vaidik (2011, 334) exalts the importance of precedent, she does allow, however, "Our legal system does not want judges to be like computers who simply intake the facts, apply the law stored in the computer, and press enter while at the same time ignoring individual circumstances." She continues, "We think about the balancing of social issues. We think, in part, with our heart when we look at a case: how do we feel about this case?; what's the right thing to do?; and what's the justice of the cause? We look through the prism of our personal and professional experiences. I may look at a criminal case, having been a former prosecutor, a little different from my colleagues, who may not have experience" (2011, 334).

Moreover, in "Neutrality, Legitimacy, and the Supreme Court: Some Intersections Between Law and Political Science," Deutsch (1968, 260–261) explains the effect formal and informal 'schooling' might have on judicial discretion:

> The Court, unlike Congress, is not a social system; the task of a Justice is far more an individual than a group endeavor; and the influence of other Justices and of the institution on a new member of the Court is correspondingly limited. To a far greater extent than is true in the case of a Congressman, therefore, the search for factors that effectively impose restraints on the discretion of the individual Justice must be carried beyond the realm of his work experience to that of his schooling, both formal and informal. Such an investigation, a branch of the study of political 'socialization,' might profitably begin with an examination of the impact of their professional training on given Justices. For example, to what extent can a particular Justice's perception of the range of discretion he can legitimately exercise be ascribed to a professional training that was primarily 'policy–oriented'?

But what are the theoretical reasons why such characteristics and experiences might matter? What are the empirical implications of such an effect? Nearly forty years ago, Scheb and Ungs (1987, 405) wrote, "The theoretical and empirical issue which has yet to be addressed effectively by political scientists is why such variation



R.V. Carman, Jr., *Making Good Law or Good Policy?*,
DOI 10.1007/978-3-319-53381-0_4

in judicial role orientations occurs." As was argued in Chap. 2, this observation still holds true today. This chapter begins, in Sect. 4.1, by building on the theory articulated in Chap. 2 to develop three models of role orientation development: one based on the institutional structures of the courts, one based on the backgrounds of judges, and one that integrates both. Empirical tests of these models of the determinants of the judicial role theory are devised in Sect. 4.2, the results of which are discussed in Sect. 4.3.

## 4.1 Role, Role Expectations, and Role Synthesization

Institutions have long been of interest to social scientists. Defined as "the rules of the game in a society or…constraints that shape human behavior" (North 1990, 3), institutions can be either formal, such as rules that individuals purposely construct; or informal, such as conventions and norms that develop naturally. Said another way, institutions are sets of rules that structure social interactions in particular ways and constrain the actions of others (Knight 1992).

Scholars of the judiciary have found clear support for the theory that institutions structure judicial behavior. Nowhere in judicial research has that theory found greater support than in the study of state courts, where institutional structures vary greatly from state to state. The absence of a discretionary docket, the length of the judicial term, and the method used to select and retain judges, for example, all affect the behavior of judges (Brace and Hall 1990, 1995, 1997; Brace et al. 2000, 2001; Hall and Brace 1994).

These findings comport very well with role theory. Role theory argues that the way individuals act within an institution differs from the way they act in non–institutional settings: that environment structures behavior. In role theoretic language, roles are the constraints imposed on individuals by an institutional structure. These roles limit, but do not eliminate, discretion in the interest of advancing organizational objectives (Gibson 1981, 292–293). "[R]ole theory provides a means of moving beyond an exclusive focus on individuals to consider the influence of the institutional constraints on decision making" (Gibson 1983, 17) because "institutions exist…to circumscribe the alternatives available to the decision–maker" (Gibson 1981, 293).

Roles do not constrain behavior alone, however. Role occupants often have their own preconceived notions of the proper role orientation. The two primary influences on these notions of the proper role orientation are the occupants' personal characteristics and professional experiences. As Hewitt (2007, 30) describes, "We humans are born into an already existing society and culture, and are quickly swept into its flow. We are surrounded by others who define reality for us, showing us the objects in their world and in some ways requiring us to make them our own." Given the influence that society and culture have on individuals, it is reasonable to suspect that a judge's personal characteristics may result in certain viewpoints that may strongly influence his or her ultimate role orientations (Wold 1974, 242).

In addition to the effect that role alters' preconceived notions have on the development of individual's role orientation, a role occupant interacts with many other individuals (or, role alters) in the course of performing in his or her position. These role alters hold normative beliefs, or role expectations, about how the role occupant ought to behave. These normative beliefs about proper role behavior, role theory explains, are also incorporated into an individual's role orientation.

Take, for example, the position of judge: It is expected that all judges are (at least somewhat) constrained by precedent, regardless of how the judge was appointed, how long the judge has served, or whether the judge serves on a trial court or an appellate court. This is because would–be judges are taught in law school and from the practice law that judges should follow precedent. In addition, relevant role alters—such as lawyers, the media, other judges, politicians, and the public—hold expectations that judges should value precedent. Of course, the extent to which these role expectations influence judicial decision–making varies. For example, relevant role alters might expect stricter adherence to precedent from a trial judge than an appellate judge; likewise for a newer precedent compared to an older one. However, the general normative belief that judges should value precedent applies to all judges and, generally speaking, judges do profess to value precedent.

When a *role conflict*, or conflicting role expectations, presents itself, the role occupant must choose to accept some role expectations and reject others.[1] Of course, not all role occupants hold the same preconceived notion of proper role behavior and not all role occupants synthesize role expectations the same way. If this happened, all of the occupants of a particular position—say, all of the judges on a particular court—would behave the same way—in the case of these judges, reach the same conclusion in a case.

Symbolic interactionists say that conduct is predicated on meaning, which is variable and emergent. Meaning is not merely handed down, but rather arises and is transformed by how people act in situations (Hewitt 2007, 27–28). Therefore, the professional experiences of a role occupant may very well have an even greater impact on role orientation. As Scheb and Ungs (1987) explain, the judicial culture supplies individuals with certain intellectual and behavioral parameters of permissibility. Individuals develop their particular role orientations within these parameters. For example, during law school, a future judge is first exposed to the professions' definition of judge. Subsequent law practice further molds the future judge's views concerning the proper judicial function. Having ascended to the bench, continued interaction with fellow judges and attorneys may reinforce the judge's role orientation or cause the judge to alter these views (Wold 1974, 242).

[1] As Preiss and Ehrlich (1966) explain, there are two types of role conflict: contradictory and contrary. *Contradictory expectations* are ones in which "all cannot be fulfilled *and* one in which all cannot be ignored" (1966, 95). Thus, in situations with contradictory exceptions, any behavior selected by the role occupant, including inaction, will fail to fulfill the role expectations of one or more role alters. *Contrary exceptions*, on the other hand, are ones that "cannot all be fulfilled, but *can* be ignored" (1966, 95). In situations with contrary expectations, while any selection among the given role expectations will not meet the approval of *some* role alters, the selection may not be construed as violating the given expectation.

In the end, there is no universally accepted judicial role orientation. Rather the process is "stochastic and is one of individuals' reacting in a variety of distinctive ways" (Gibson 1983, 17) to their role, to the expectations of role alters, and to their own belief about the proper behavior given their characteristics and experiences. Because the position of judge is incredibly complex, "judges' beliefs about the limits of proper behavior are also complex" (Gibson 1981, 302). 'Proper' in this context does not refer to the policy content of judicial decisions, but rather to the process of decision–making and, in particular, the kinds of stimuli that should influence decisions (Gibson 1978, 918).

## 4.2 Research Design

Role orientations are the product of synthesizing institutional rules, one's own preconceived idea of the proper role orientation, and the role expectations of others. This chapter examines the effect that these influences have on the role orientations of state high court judges. The main data for this study was collected from a mail survey of the entire population of state high court judges. Chapter 3 details the steps taken to design and implement this survey.[2]

Following logically from the conceptualization of judicial role orientation adopted in Chap. 2, and grounded firmly in the judicial 'activism' literature, this study operationalizes judges' role orientations as being somewhere on a continuum that ranges from 'restraintist' to 'activist.' A 'restraintist' judge is one who believes that precedent, the strict construction of constitutions, and deference to legislative intent are extremely important decisional criteria. 'Activists,' on the other hand, are judges who give greater decisional weight to personal attitudes, values, and case outcomes (Gibson 1983, 17–18).

The source of the dependent variable for this analysis are a series of six statements, a slightly modified version of Gibson's (1981) proposed questionnaire, in which each judge was asked to indicate the degree (on a four–point Likert scale)[3,4] to which he or she agrees with the following six statements:

1. A good judge is one who sticks as closely as possible to precedents.
2. Judges should be allowed great discretion in decision–making in order to ensure that their decisions are "just."

[2] In addition, Chap. 3 explores the general survey results.

[3] For more information about the origins of the Likert scale, see Likert (1932).

[4] To discourage what was anticipated to be the frequent use of what would amount to a meaningless response, no neutral response option was presented. Instead, a "forced choice" survey scale was adopted (Allen and Seaman 2007). In a "forced choice" survey scale, the presented response options are strongly disagree, disagree, agree, or strongly agree. While it is *possible* that a few survey respondents might truly be neutral to one of the six statements, it seemed more likely that many non–truly neutral survey respondents would check the neutral box out of political considerations and thus would bias the analyses.

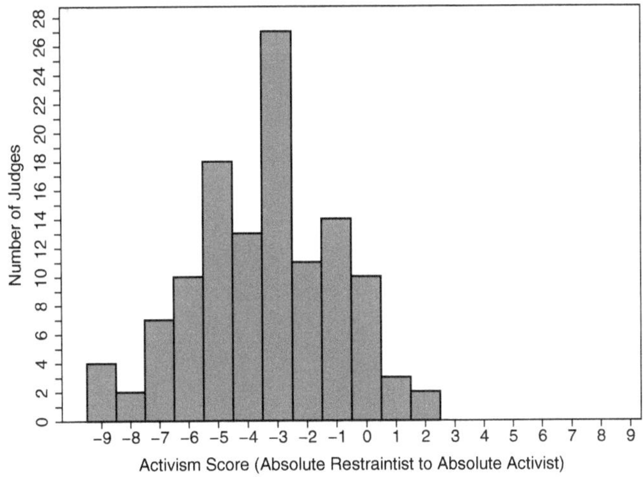


**Fig. 4.1** Frequency of judge by 'activism' score

3. It is wrong for a judge to allow his or her personal philosophy to influence his or her decisions.
4. Precedents are rarely conclusive; usually a judge can find a precedent that supports his or her own point of view.
5. Precedents and statutes are the main factors that should influence judges' decisions.
6. It is just as legitimate to make a decision and then find the precedent as it is to find the precedent and then make the decision.

Following Gibson's (1981) logic, affirmative responses to statements 1, 3, and 5 indicate that a judge's role orientation is on the 'restraintist' end of the spectrum, while affirmative responses to statements 2, 4, and 6 indicate that a judge's role orientation is on the 'activist' side. For this analysis, the exact placement of the judges on the 'activist–restraintist' spectrum was determined by aggregating their responses, such that a −9 is an absolute 'restraintist' and a +9 is an absolute 'activist.'[5]

Figure 4.1 presents the frequency of judges on the 'restraintist–activist' continuum. While the responses are skewed to the 'restraintist' end of the spectrum such that the modal score is −3 and the most 'activist' judge is scored +2, the data does resemble a normal distribution. Moreover, given the general expectation that precedent should be a crucial judicial decision–making criteria, the skewness of these

[5] Analyses using two alternative specifications of this variable are presented in Tables 4.3 and 4.4. In the first, the 'activism' score was recoded into three equally–sized categories, such that an 'activism' score of −9, −8, −7, −6, and −5 was coded as −1, an 'activism' score of −4 and −3 was coded as a 0, and an 'activism' score of −2, −1, 0, 1, and 2 was coded as 1. In the second, the 'activism' score was dichotomized so that judges who were on the positive side of the 'activism' spectrum were coded as 1 and judges who were on the 'restraint' side of the 'activism' spectrum were coded as 0.

**Table 4.1** Summary statistics with associated expectations

| Variable | Expectation | Mean/mode | Std. dev. | Range |
|---|---|---|---|---|
| Dependent variable | | | | |
| Judge's 'activism' score | N/A | −3.41 | 2.44 | −9–2 |
| Institutional structure | | | | |
| Judge must stand for reelection/retention | + | 1 | 0.42 | 0–1 |
| Judge must be reappointed by gov. or leg. | – | 0 | 0.37 | 0–1 |
| Court's professionalism score | – | 0.57 | 0.15 | 0.3–1.0 |
| Judge's background | | | | |
| Judge's ideological score | – | −0.07 | 0.81 | −1.5–1.5 |
| Judge's religiousness | + | 5.09 | 1.54 | 1–7 |
| Years of service in prosecutor's office | – | 1.97 | 4.03 | 0–18 |
| Years of service in public defender's office | + | 0.38 | 2.20 | 0–22 |
| Experience as trial court judge | + | 1 | 0.50 | 0–1 |

*Source* Retention method come from American Judicature Society (2013). Judiciary professionalism scores are Squire's (2008) Salary, Staff Size, and Docket Score. Ideology scores are Bonica and Woodruff's (2012). All other data are from the survey responses

findings are not surprising. In all, as they include at least one survey respondent, 47 of the 52 high courts are represented in the data.[6] Summary statistics with associated expectations for each variable are presented in Table 4.1.

Literature suggests that the institutional structure within which a state high court judge operates affects his or her decision–making. Langer (2003, 66) argues, "The preferences of other actors also might curtail judicial behavior more when institutional rules governing tenure security increase the electoral vulnerability of justices. Justices operating in states where they are retained by the legislature and governor, for example, might be more responsive to the preferences of these government actors. Similarly, justices retained via popular elections might be more responsive to the preferences of the state citizenry or special interest." Empirical evidence supports this contention. For example, Choi et al. (2007) find that elected judges behave like politicians (by providing service to their voters), while appointed judges behave like professionals (by focusing on their long–term legacy as creators of precedent).

Many authors have tended to suppose either a direct connection between institutional structure and judicial behavior,[7] or a more complex interplay between institutional structure, judicial preference, and case facts.[8] However, role theory explains that a judges' role orientation comes, in part, from the institution within which the judge finds him or herself. The institutional rules will help determine the stimuli that the judge feels can legitimately be allowed to influence his or her decision and, in the case of conflict among influences, what priorities to assign to each stimuli.

[6]Because Texas and Oklahoma have separate high courts, one for criminal matters and one for all other matters, there are actually 52 state high courts.

[7]See, e.g., Brace and Hall (1990) and Brace et al. (2001).

[8]See, e.g., Brace and Hall (1995, 1997) and Hall and Brace (1994).

Therefore, because of the impact institutional structure has on the development of an individual's role orientation, we should see judges in similar institutions possess similar, though not identical, role orientations.

To evaluate the effect that institutional structure has on state high court judges' role orientations, a series of three variables was created. The first two, *popularControl* and *reappointment* capture the method adopted by a state to retain its judges.[9,10] The dichotomous *popularControl* variable was coded such that a 0 indicated that the judge was not subjected to either partisan or non–partisan reelection, or a retention election and a 1 indicated that the judge was subjected to one of these retention methods. A total of 103 of the 134 survey respondents were subjected to what is termed here as popular control.

State high court judges enjoy high reelection and retention rates. Indeed, from 1990–2004, an astonishing 85% of state high court judges running for reelection and 98% of state high court judges running for retention were successful (Bonneau and Hall 2009, Table 4.4). However, as has been reported by, among others, Wold and Culver (1987), high court judges are more vulnerable to electoral defeat on the basis of their decisions than other state judges. This could be because, among other factors, the decisions of the state high courts: (1) are broader reaching, as they affect the whole state; (2) are more important, as they touch on controversial and salient issues such as the death penalty, same–sex marriage, school funding, etc.; and (3) are more likely to be known by the voters because state high court decisions are covered by the local and/or national media more often than state trial and intermediate appellate court decisions.

Despite this high reelection rate, from 1980 through 2000, state high court judges in states with partisan elections were more likely to be challenged than members of the U.S. House of Representatives (Hall 2007, 182). Likewise, state high court judges in states with partisan and nonpartisan elections are more often defeated in their reelection bid than members of the U.S. House of Representatives (Hall 2007, 183).

All this has led scholars to posit that concern about retaining their judgeship might influence the policy choices that state high court judges make (Baum 1994). Research lends support for this contention. In their study of the effect that judicial elections have on judges' votes to reverse capital punishment sentences, which appears in Streb's (2007) edited volume on judicial elections, Brace and Boyea (2007, 192) conclude that the lowest rates of capital punishment reversals (20%) occurred in states in which judges were elected by a public most supportive of the death penalty. In contrast, the highest rates of capital punishment reversals (29%) occurred in states in which judges were appointed and the public was greatly in favor of the death penalty. This supports the role theoretic presumption that institutional structures define which role

---

[9]Retention methods were determined by consulting American Judicature Society (2013).

[10]For the analyses that follow, the excluded category is judges with life tenure, or life tenure until a mandatory retirement age.

alters' expectations must be considered. The authors also find that judges are most responsive to the public immediately before an election (Brace and Boyea 2007, 194).[11]

Moreover, role theoretic scholars have found a relationship between selection system and judges' role orientations. For example, Glick and Vines (1969) find that New Jersey judges are alone in their majority adoption of the 'law–maker' role orientation and Louisiana in its almost exclusive adoption of the 'law–interpreter' role orientation.[12] In role theoretic language, for judges who are subject to popular control, the voters are relevant role alters. As role alters, the voters preferences must be weighted accordingly by these judges. As these voters will not care whether precedent needs to be overturned, or the legislature deferred to, in order to reach the preferred outcome of a case, judges who are retained through popular control will be more likely to have 'activist' role orientations than judges who have life tenure and are thereby insulated from this external pressure. As Baum (1994, 751) suggests, "judges might try to appeal to the public, in order to ensure reelection."

The second institutional structure variable, the dichotomous *reappointment* variable, was coded such that a 0 indicated that the judge was not subjected to either an executive or legislative reappointment and a 1 indicated that the judge was subjected to one of these reappointments. A total of 21 of the 134 survey respondents were subjected to executive or legislative reappointment.

Just as the voters are relevant role alters for judges who are subjected to popular control, the executive and/or legislature are relevant role alters, and their preferences weighted as such, for those judges who must be reappointed to remain in office. One of the dimensions that role orientation has been operationalized here is whether a 'good' judge is one who defers to the political branches of government. Indeed, a 'restraintist' judge has, in part, been defined here as one who defers to the political branches of government. As such, it is expected that state high court judges who are retained through reappointment will be more likely to have 'restraintist' role orientations than judges who serve for life.

The third institutional structure variable, *professionalismScore*, indicates the professionalism of the court. The *professionalismScore*, developed by Squire (2008, 225), gauges the "institutional capacity [of a court] to generate and evaluate information." Adopted from his work on the professionalism of state legislatures,[13] *professionalismScore*, which ranges from 0.253 to 1.004, incorporates measures of judicial salary, staff support, and docket control.[14]

---

[11]See, also, Hall (1987, 1992, 1995).

[12]The authors do note that, since they only examined four states (two appointive and two elective), the results could be an artifact of the state itself and not the appointment scheme.

[13]See Squire (1992, 2007).

[14]Choi et al. (2009) provide an alternative ranking of state judiciaries. However, because a constituent component of that variable is a measure of judges' ideology and, consistent with expectations from the literature, this model includes a measure of judges' ideology, Squire's (2008) scores are used to avoid issues of multicollinearity. Squire's (2008) scores are also preferable in that a constituent component of their measure is extent to which the court controls its own docket.

Squire (2008) incorporates salary into this measure of professionalization based on the assumption that higher pay will attract and retain better qualified judges. The salary component of the professionalization measure controls for both the raw salary of the judges, which range from a high of $175,575 in California to a low of $95,000 in West Virginia, as well as the wage premium compared to the mean salary of lawyers in the state paid to high court judges, which range from a low of 59% in Rhode Island to a high of 101% in Utah.[15]

Because a court's ability to evaluate information and produce legal opinions should increase with the number of law clerks assigned to each judge to provide research and writing assistance, Squire (2008) measures staff support as the number of law clerks assigned to each judge. The number of clerks range from less than one clerk per judge in Alabama to more than five clerks per judge in Pennsylvania.

Finally, the third component of Squire's (2008) professionalization measure is demands on time. In his earlier work on state legislatures, Squire (2007) used the number of days each legislature was in session each year to determine the ability of that legislature to develop and evaluate policy. As all state high courts are full–time institutions, the analog, "may be the extent to which an appellate court can focus its attention on the most pressing legal problems brought before it" (Squire 2008, 226). "Docket control gives an appellate court the ability to manage the number of cases it hears and to select cases that it deems the most important to decide. Appellate courts that can largely determine which cases they hear have a greater ability to craft their decisions compared with appellate courts that cannot pick and choose" (2008, 226).

Squire (2008) devised two different ways to measure docket control. The first indicates whether the state high court's jurisdiction was discretionary in the seven areas of case law heard by state high courts: administrative agency, civil, disciplinary, juvenile, interlocutory, non–capital crime, and original proceedings. This created a scale running from 0 if none of the case areas was discretionary, to 7 if all of the case areas was discretionary. The second reports the total number of mandatory cases filed with each state's high court and the total number of discretionary petitions filed in 2004. These figures where then used to calculate the percentage of each state high court's docket composed of discretionary cases. Scores on the measure of docket control using the percentage of discretionary cases range from 0 in two states to 1 in four states, with a median of 0.795.

Given the two measures of salary and two measures of docket control, Squire (2008) creates four versions of his professionalism score. The measures are highly correlated: the lowest correlation is 0.879 ($p < 0.000$, two–tailed), between the index with salary and discretionary cases and the index with the salary premium and docket control, while the highest correlation is 0.980 ($p < 0.000$, two–tailed), between the two indices with the discretionary cases component (2008, 228). Following conventional application, this analysis adopts the first, which uses salary, staff size, and

[15] Squire (2008) obtained the mean lawyer salary using data gathered from the U.S. Department of Labor, the Bureau of Labor Statistics, and the November 2004 State Occupational Employment and Wage Estimates.

docket score.[16] In calculating these measures, Squire (2008) used the United States Supreme Court as a baseline against which to measure the professionalization of each state's high court. Thus a state high court scored 1.000 is identically professional to the United States Supreme Court and a lower score indicates that a state high court is less professional than the United States Supreme Court.

As the United States Supreme Court is the benchmark for Squire's (2008) score, we can look to that Court for guidance as to how 'activist' similar courts might be. Howard and Segal (2004) find that the U.S. Supreme Court is reluctant to exercise its power of judicial review, and therefore is 'restraintist' in its actions. That Court grants only 21.4% of litigant requests to overturn a state or federal law as unconstitutional (Howard and Segal 2004, 134).[17] The authors suppose that "excessively frequent assertions of judicial review…can lead to a lack of respect for the Court, political outcry to impeach activist judges, attempts to curtail the Court's power through restrictions on appellate jurisdiction, and even attempts to alter the composition of the Court itself" (Howard and Segal 2004, 142). Therefore, as the U.S. Supreme Court is 'restraintist' in its striking down of law as unconstitutional, it is expected that the more professional a judiciary is the more likely that court's members are to have a 'restraintist' role orientation.

As to the effect judges' backgrounds have on the judicial role orientation, a series of five variables were created. The first, *ideology*, captures the ideology of the state high court judges. To do so, ideological scores developed by Bonica and Woodruff (2012) are used. These scores range from −1.52 (most liberal) to 1.51 (most conservative) with a mean value of −0.07 and a standard deviation of 0.81. These scores are constructed using publicly available campaign contribution data to place judges in a common ideological space with other federal and state officials using a step–wise procedure.

> First, if a justice ran for election, we assign an ideal point based on her CFscore received as a candidate. If a justice has not run for judicial office, we look to whether he campaigned for a different elected office during his political career. If the justice has not run for elected office, we search for the justice in the database of individual contributors…Finally, if the justice was appointed, but has neither given nor received campaign contributions, we assign a score for the justice based on the CFscores of the appointing governor or legislative body. For justices appointed by the legislature, we assign ideal points based on the CFscore of the median member of the relevant legislative bodies involved in the appointment process (2012, 8–9).

These scores are preferable to the PAJID scores developed by Brace et al. (2000). The PAJID scores, developed using Berry et al.'s (1998) state elite and citizen ideological scores which were in turn developed using the ADA interest group ratings of each state's congressional delegation, are "so far divorced from the target actor [that

---

[16] Alternative analyses using the other three versions of the professionalism score are presented in Tables 4.5, 4.6, and 4.7.

[17] Not surprisingly, the U.S. Supreme Court receives more requests to strike state laws than it does requests to strike federal laws and it does, in fact, strike a greater percent of state laws (25.7%) than federal laws (10.1%) (Howard and Segal 2004, Table 1).

they] make[] for extremely noisy measures that prove inadequate for studying the effects of judicial selection and judicial reforms" (Bonica and Woodruff 2012, 2).

These scores are also preferable to the self–identified partisanship data collected by the survey questionnaire on several counts.[18] First, while 10 judges refused to provide their partisan affiliation, only one judge is missing an ideological score in Bonica and Woodruff's (2012) data. This results in fewer judges being excluded from this analysis. Second, many judges might not have accurately indicated their partisanship.[19] As such, utilizing observable behavior—in this case the campaign contributions made to judges or by judges—is preferable to questionable self–reported data.

Wold (1974) found a strong relationship between a judge's ideology and their role orientation.[20] "Political conservatives uniformly adopted the law–interpreter position, and political moderates were strongly attracted to the eclectic position. More political liberals adopted the lawmaker orientation than did the members of either of the other two groups…" (1974, 247–248).[21] Likewise, in his study of the role orientations of judges on three U.S. Courts of Appeals, Howard (1977) found support for the contention that judges' ideology affects their role orientation. "Four of the five Innovators identified themselves as having been political liberals before becoming federal judges; only one of nine Interpreters did so. A single Innovator called himself a former political conservative, perhaps as a joke. Otherwise, the large majority were men in the middle, self–styled moderates before becoming jurists, who likewise straddled the conflict over lawmaking" (1977, 924–925).[22]

Moreover, an often repeated belief held by some politicians and some in the popular media is that judicial activism is only carried out by liberal judges.[23] Indeed, liberal and 'activist' have, for some, become synonymous. Therefore, if these results and this contention are true, then we should expect that judges who identify as Democrats should be more likely to identify as 'activists' and judges who identify as Republicans should be more likely to identify as 'restraintists.'

---

[18]Survey respondents were asked a slightly modified version of the American National Election Studies (2012) partisanship question: "Generally speaking, do you consider yourself a Democrat, a Republican, or something else?" To try to gently persuade survey respondents to supply a party identification (something it was believed judges might be reluctant to report), the response choices did not include an option for independent or unaffiliated but rather were limited to Democrat, Republican, and Other. However, any written in survey response that indicated that the respondent felt they were independent or nonpartisan was coded as Independent/Nonpartisan.

[19]See Chap. 2 for a more elaborate discussion of this topic.

[20]But, see, Scheb et al. (1989).

[21]Wold (1974) defined 'law–interpreters' as judges that "perceived their job to be almost solely one of following legal precedent and the will of the legislature," 'eclectics' as judges that "felt the function of the court depended upon the particular case before it," and 'lawmaker' as judges that were not "averse to creating new law when convinced that circumstances warranted it" (1974, 240).

[22]Howard (1977) defines 'innovators' as judges who "felt obliged to make law whenever the opportunity occurs" and 'interpreter' as judges who felt "judicial lawmaking should be held to a minimum" (1977, 919–920).

[23]See, for example, Levin (2005).

Some authors have supposed an effect for religion on judicial decision–making. For example, Gryski and Main (1986, 530) hypothesize that "judges of fundamentalist faiths [are] least likely to support a sex discrimination claim, on the grounds that many of those religions have unambiguously voiced their opposition to the equal rights amendment."[24] In terms the judicial role orientation, only one work explores religion's effect. Wold (1974, 243), without explanation, states that the more "innovative role orientations (lawmaker or eclectic) would be closely associated with…affiliation with the…Roman Catholic or Jewish denomination." He finds support for this supposition. "Protestant judges tended to take a much more restrictive view of their role than either Catholic or Jewish jurist" (1974, 243).

While there are theoretical reasons to suspect that denomination might have an effect on judicial decision–making, (see, for example, Blake (2012), Songer and Tabrizi (1999), and Yarnold (2000)), at least in particular issue areas, there is no a priori reason to suspect, *ceteris paribus*, that a Roman Catholic, Protestant, etc., is more 'activist' than a member of any other faith. This is not to say that religion could not affect role orientation, rather that there is no theoretically–grounded reason to expect its effect is through denomination. Wold's (1974) findings might very well be an artifact of his data. "Every Protestant who took the law–interpreter position also described himself as a political conservative. Over one–half of the Catholic and Jewish judges were political liberals, and none of the members of either denomination termed himself a conservative" (1974, 243). A better way to test for religions' effect on the judicial role orientation might be through religiousness.

The second background variable, *religiousness*, gauges how religious each of the high court judges consider themselves to be. The judges were asked, "Apart from weddings and funerals, how often do you attend religious services?" The response choices were: every day, almost every day, every week, almost every week, once or twice a month, a few times a year, and never. The variable was coded such that a 1 indicated daily attendance, a 2 indicated attendance almost every day, a 3 indicated attendance every week, a 4 indicated attendance almost every week, a 5 indicated attendance once or twice a month, a 6 indicated attendance a few times a year, and a 7 indicated attendance never. In all, 126 out of 134 survey respondents answered this question.[25] Few survey respondents (0.8%) attend church every day, none attend church almost every day, though the most report attending services every week (23%) or almost every week (14.3%). Nearly one–third of survey respondents (27.8%) report attending church a few times a year and over 22% never attend services.

As argued by Clark and Dawson (1996, 359), "personal religiousness is an apt starting point for finding differences in moral judgement." "For the believer, there is little room for rejection of [religious authority and revealed truth]. Acceptance on the

---

[24]See, also, for example, Nagel (1961) and Ulmer (1973).

[25]Wherever possible, missing survey response data was obtained through judicial biographies, newspaper articles, and professional directories. Experiential survey responses for 14 judges were located through these means. The frequency of church attendance, however, is not something that can be located through other means. As such, to account for the effect that these missing values might have on the model, an alternative model without this variable was specified. The results of this model are presented in Table 4.8.

basis of divine origin is a condition for membership and participation in the assembly of believers" (De George 1986, 424). "The nonbeliever, however, is not similarly influenced" (Clark and Dawson 1996, 359). Given the role that religiousness has on moral judgment, it is expected that the more religious a judge is, the more results–oriented he or she might be (particularly on social issues where morality comes into play, such as abortion, the death penalty, and same–sex marriage). Said another way, judges with high religiosity will be guided more by their moral judgement in their decision–making than a sense of upholding precedent or deferring to the political branches.[26] As such, as a judge's self–identified religiousness increases, so to should his or her 'activism.'

As Wold (1974, 242) describes, "Judges' early lives, their training and professional careers may have instilled in them certain viewpoints regarding questions of public policy and may have strongly influenced their ultimate role concepts…Their subsequent law practices may have further molded their views concerning the proper judicial function." The remaining four background variables attempt to capture the effects that these early career experiences might have on the development of judges' role orientations.

The third and fourth background variables, *yrsDistAttOff* and *yrsPubDefOff*, indicate the number of years a judge reported to have served in a prosecutor's office and a public defender's office, respectively. A total of 49 judges had experience in the prosecutor's office and 22 judges had experience in the public defender's office before joining the bench.

In his treatise on the role of public defender, Nunn (1995, 786–787) writes, "The image and appearance of the prosecutor is not happenstance. It is partially a function of seeking to reflect majoritarianism and to avoid identification with any 'special interest group'…The image that the prosecutor projects embraces and endorses the mainstream, and thereby, embraces and endorses hierarchy and power." On the other hand,

> "While public defenders have the prestige of being members of the bar—they are respected to that degree by court officials, witnesses, and laypeople—that prestige is tempered by two factors: they represent 'criminals,' and they are the opponents of the state…Unlike the case with prosecutors, it is not unusual to find flamboyant and eccentric personalities among the ranks of public defenders…Rather than embrace the status quo, the public defender purports to stand somewhere outside of the mainstream. The public defender projects the image of the anti–establishmentarian rebel more so than that of the efficient and professional public servant" (Nunn 1995, 788)

Given the former's role orientation that includes valuing hierarchy and power, it is expected that service in a prosecutor's office would increase the likelihood that a judge would have a 'restraintist' role orientation. Conversely, given the latter's role orientation that includes being an anti–establishmentarian rebel, it is expected that service in public defender's office would increase the likelihood that a judge would have an 'activist' role orientation.

---

[26]It is also possible that judges who attend church services regularly have built more social capital and trust in the system.

Baum (1997, 63) reports that "[p]otential judges' orientations may differ with their career experiences. Lawyers who spend their whole pre–judicial careers in legal practice might tend to think about legal policy from a legal perspective, while those who have devoted themselves to politics and government might be more policy–oriented." Yet, surprisingly, little work on the judicial role orientation has anticipated the impact that previously serving on a trial court might have on a state high court judge's role orientation.

Therefore, given the theoretical reasons why we might expect an influence from past experiences, the final background variable is *trialCtExp*. This variable indicates whether the judge had previously served on a federal, state, or local trial court. The dichotomous *trialCtExp* variable was coded such that a 0 indicated the judge had no such experience and a 1 indicated that the judge had experience in said office. In all, 69 of the 134 judges served as a trial court judge prior to joining the high court. It is expected that service as a trial court judge would make a judge more likely to be an 'activist' because his or her new–found freedom from the norm of precedent enforcement from courts above.

## 4.3 Results and Discussion

Models were constructed to test the effect that institutional structure and a judge's background have on the judge's 'Activism' Score, both as separate models and as an integrated model. As Long (1997, 114) states, "When a variable is ordinal, its categories can be ranked from low to high, but the distances between adjacent categories are unknown." Powers and Xie (2000, 201) explain, "Examples of ordinal qualitative data include the Likert scales, in which responses on questions take such categories as strongly disagree, disagree, neutral, agree, or strongly agree." Though researchers often treat ordinal dependent variables as if they were interval variables and estimate an OLS regression, "this involves the implicit assumption that the intervals between adjacent categories are equal" (Long 1997, 115). Rather than make what would be a dubious assumption in this case, following the advice of Long (1997), a series of three ordered logistic regression models was estimated. The results from these models are presented in Table 4.2.

The column titled "Institutional Model" describes the results the institutional structure variables alone have on judicial 'activism.' Two of the three variables are statistically significant when the effects of judges' backgrounds are not controlled for. First, and as expected, standing for reelection or retention election makes a judge more likely to have an 'activist' role orientation. This is certainly consistent with the literature on judicial elections shaping judicial behavior.[27] The average effect of

[27] See, for example, Hall (1987, 1992, 1995) and Brace and Boyea (2007).

**Table 4.2** Ordered logistic regression of 'activism' score

| Variable | Institutional model | Background model | Combined model |
|---|---|---|---|
| Institutional structure | | | |
| Judge must stand for reelection/retention[a] | 1.073*** | | 1.643*** |
| | (0.341) | | (0.463) |
| Judge must be reappointed by gov. or leg.[a] | 1.062* | | 1.231 |
| | (0.642) | | (0.797) |
| Court's professionalism score | −1.612 | | −2.869*** |
| (Salary, Docket score, and Staff) | (1.140) | | (1.113) |
| Judge's background | | | |
| Judge's ideological score | | −0.510** | −0.675*** |
| | | (0.217) | (0.206) |
| Judge's religiousness | | 0.126 | 0.173 |
| | | (0.121) | (0.123) |
| Years of service in prosecutor's office | | 0.051 | 0.062* |
| | | (0.036) | (0.033) |
| Years of service in public defender's office | | −0.231*** | −0.204** |
| | | (0.085) | (0.088) |
| Experience as trial court judge | | 0.540 | 0.820** |
| | | (0.350) | (0.346) |
| Model diagnostics | | | |
| Number of observations | 120 | 112 | 112 |
| Wald $chi^2$ | 11.860 | 22.23 | 48.820 |
| Probability > $chi^2$ | 0.008 | 0.000 | 0.000 |
| McKelvey and Zavoina's $R^2$ | 0.045 | 0.148 | 0.240 |

*Note* Numbers in parentheses are robust standard errors clustered on state. $^{*}p < 0.1$, $^{**}p < 0.05$, $^{***}p < 0.01$

[a]The excluded category is judges with life tenure, or life tenure until a mandatory retirement age

this variable is such that a judge who is subject to popular control has a 7% higher 'Activism' Score than a judge who is not subjected to popular control.[28]

The other variable in the "Institutional Model" that is statistically significant is the reappointment variable. Needing to be reappointed by a governor or legislature makes a judge more likely to have an 'activist' role orientation. The average effect of this variable is such that a judge who is subject to reappointment has a 2% higher 'Activism' Score than a judge who is not subjected to reappointment. This is contrary to the expectation laid out above. One possible explanation for this finding is that governors and legislators might value the positive electoral consequences of their reappointing judges popular with the public (those who are results–oriented) more so

[28]Discrete change effects were calculated for each statistically significant variable by estimating the difference in the predicted value that changing the variable from its minimum value to its maximum value, holding all other independent variables at their means.

than governors and legislators value judges who defer to their will. The presence of an intermediate appellate court and the state's professionalism score are not statistically significant in the "Institutional Model."

The column titled "Background Model" describes the results that judges' personal characteristics and professional experiences have on their role orientation. Two of the five background variables are statistically significant when institutional effects are not controlled for. First, and as expected, liberal judges are more likely to have an 'activist' role orientation than conservative judges. This is consistent with the role orientation literature described above.[29] The average effect of this variable is such that the most liberal judge has a 4% higher 'Activism' Score than the most conservative judge.

Second, service as a public defender has a significant effect on judges' role orientations. However, contrary to expectation, such service makes a judge more likely to have a 'restraintist' role orientation. The average effect of this variable is such that a judge who has the longest experience of serving in the public defender's office has a 21% lower 'Activism' Score. One explanation for these findings is that criminal practice is so driven by rules and procedures that the expectations that seem rational on their face do not apply. In particular, it is quite possible that the role performed by prosecutors and public defenders are so well proscribed by criminal law and court rules that this experience cannot affect judges' role orientations in the way that we might otherwise expect.

The final column describes the results for the "Combined Model" that integrates both institutional and background variables. Results in this model indicate that: popular control, judges' ideology, and service in the public defender's office remain statistically significant; reappointment is no longer statistically significant; and the court's professionalism score, service in the prosecutor's office, and experience as a trial court judge become statistically significant.

As to popular control, the effect remains positive. The average effect is such that a judge who is subject to popular control is 7% more 'activist' than a judge who is not subject to popular control. As hypothesized above, the more professional a state's judiciary is the more likely its judges are to be 'restraintist.' The average effect of the professionalism score is such that a judge in the most professional judiciary has a 6% lower 'Activism' Score than a judge in the least professional judiciary.

In the "Combined Model," all of the background variables are statistically significant except the one signifying the judges' religiousness. Ideology continues to exert a negative effect. The average effect of this variable is such that the most liberal judge has a 4% higher 'Activism' Score than the most conservative judge. Service as a prosecutor or public defender, in the "Combined Model," are both statistically significant. Service as prosecutor has the average effect such that a judge who has the most experience has a 2% higher 'Activism' Score than a judge who does not have this experience. Service as a public defender has the average effect such that a judge who has this experience has a 21% lower 'Activism' Score.

---

[29]Though judicial role theory scholars anticipate this result, it should be noted that the true direction of the causal arrow is unknown. That is: are liberals 'activists' or are 'activists' liberals?

When institutional variables are controlled for, trial court experience becomes statistically significant. As expected from above, judges who had previously served on the trial court, now free from the expectation that they will faithfully apply precedent, are more likely to have an 'activist' role orientation. The average effect such that a judge who has this experience has a 2% higher 'Activism' Score.

Overall the "Background Model" (with a McKelvey and Zavoina's $R^2$ of 0.148 and a probability of obtaining a Chi Square test statistic of 22.23 at 0.00%) explains much more of the variation in the judicial role orientation than does the "Institutional Model" (with a McKelvey and Zavoina's $R^2$ of 0.045 and a probability of obtaining a Chi Square test statistic of 11.86 at 0.8%).[30] This would seem to indicate that, despite theoretical reasons and previous empirical findings, a judge's role orientation is formed before a judge joins the bench. Said another way, the judge's own perception of proper influences on judicial decision–making inspires their role orientation before institutional structures can affect their role orientation. This is quite a novel finding.

## 4.4 Conclusion

Scheb and Ungs (1987, 405) write, "The theoretical and empirical issue which has yet to be addressed effectively by political scientists is why such variation in judicial role orientations occurs." This chapter set out to address this deficiency, both theoretically and empirically. Building on previous chapters, theory explained that a judges' role orientations are the product of synthesizing institutional rules, one's own preconceived idea of the proper role orientation, and the role expectations of others.

Empirically, it was demonstrated that a model incorporating elements of both institutional structure and judges' background characteristics and professional experiences is compelling in its ability to explain the judicial role orientation. Specifically,

[30] As Hagle and Mitchell (1992, 762–764) note, "One of the shortcomings of probit and logit analyses is the relative lack of diagnostics that regression analysts have come to expect...McKelvey and Zavoina (1975, 105–106) specifically assume the existence of an underlying unobserved interval–level continuous dependent variable that, if it could be measured, would satisfy [the preferable] linear model...In practice, the latent dependent variable is unavailable. The unavailability of the latent dependent variable has precluded a meaningful comparison of the pseudo–$R^2$s because the natural benchmark—the OLS $R^2$ generated from the underlying interval–level dependent variable—is also unavailable from the empirical data." To determine which pseudo $R^2$ most closely resembles the OLS $R^2$, Hagle and Mitchell (1992) conduct Monte Carlo simulations on four pseudo $R^2$. Following these simulations, the authors conclude "McKelvey–Zavoina and the corrected Aldrich–Nelson come the closest to satisfying the theoretical expectations and perform quite well" (1992, 782). Moreover, relying on this simulation as well as one from Windmeijer (1995), Long and Freese (2006, 196), write, in their chapter on ordered logistic regression models, "McKelvey and Zavoina's $R^2$ most closely approximates the $R^2$ obtained by fitting the linear regression model on the underlying latent variable." The authors go on to create a Stata command that calculates the McKelvey and Zavoina's $R^2$ for ordered logistic regression models and present it as the mode of calculating goodness–of–fit for ordered logistic regressions. Following this advice, goodness–of–fit in this chapter is presented as McKelvey and Zavoina's $R^2$.

and consistently, subjecting judges to reelections or retention elections and judges' ideology, and experience as a public defender help shape a judge's role orientation.

However, a few potential concerns should be addressed. First, although the response rate is quite good for an elite survey, it does not eliminate the possibility of response rate bias. For example, it could be possible that more 'restraintists' responded to the survey since they are, by definition, more predisposed to following rules. There is no way to determine if the skew toward 'restraintist' noted above is indicative of the fact that there are more 'restraintist' state high court judges or that more 'restraintist' state high court judges responded to the survey. That being said, steps were taken, and reported in Chap. 3, to compare the survey respondents to the entire population of state high court judges on all characteristics where population–level data were available. These comparisons revealed no significant bias.

Moreover, from a survey methodological perspective, as Flango et al. (1975, 280) report,

> In any survey research project, there is always the danger of possible respondent self–selection, and for this reason the conclusions obtained from these data should be treated with some caution. However, recent empirical evidence indicates that concern over bias, presumed to be inherent in every sample with a low rate of response, may be exaggerated, particularly if the population under study is homogeneous. Judges constitute a peculiar, homogeneous subgroup within any national population. After comparing many studies involving differences between respondents and nonrespondents, Leslie (1972) concluded: '...researchers surveying issues directly related to homogeneous groups should not be overly concerned about the percentage of questionnaire returns. Representativeness will most likely be excellent. This presumes, of course, that enough responses are gained to meet statistical assumptions.'

Relatedly, though 134 state high court judges responded to the survey questionnaire, several questionnaires were returned incomplete. The questions most often left incomplete were those related to this chapter's dependent variable: the judges' role orientations. Given these incomplete responses, the number of observations with complete data range from a high of 120 for the "Institution Model" to a low of 112 (because of missing religiousness data) for the "Background Model" and "Combined Model."[31] Some might raise concerns about the results of the models presented in this chapter given the number of observations and the number of independent variables.

To this end, Hamilton (1992, 225), writes, "[M]aximum likelihood estimates of logit parameters should, theoretically, have the desirable property of unbiasedness, efficiency, and normality—in large enough samples. There exist several rules of thumb for what constitutes a large–enough sample (for example, $n - K$ should exceed 100).[32] The issue of sample size is tricky, however, because the statistical property of logit estimates depend not just on the overall sample size but also on the number of cases with a given combination of $X$ and $Y$ values.[33] Skewed $Y$ distributions

[31] To determine whether these missing data exerted a significant influence on these models, auxiliary analyses excluding this variable were run. The results of that model are presented in Table 4.8.

[32] That is, the number of observations minus the number of independent variables should exceed 100.

[33] In this discussion, Hamilton (1992) uses $X$ to indicate an independent variable and $Y$ to indicate a dependent variable.

are particularly troublesome. A sample of 200 cases, but only 5 cases with $Y = 1$, provides little information about the partial effects of several $X$ variables."

In the present analysis, the model with the fewest number of observations and the greatest number of independent variables is the "Combined Model," with 112 observations and eight independent variables. The difference between these figures exceeds the 'rule of thumb' offered by Hamilton (1992). In addition, though the dependent variable is skewed to the 'restraintist' end of the spectrum such that the modal score is $-3$ and the most 'activist' judge is scored $+2$, as reported above, the data does resemble a normal distribution. This should give us some comfort in the models' general findings and the models' goodness–of–fit measures, particularly when the McKelvey and Zavoina's $R^2$ shows that the "Combined Model" explains 24% of the variation in the dependent variable.

Surely the measures of role orientation used here are not perfect. As one survey respondent wrote, "The questions...do not lend themselves to bright line answers." However, these measures fit squarely within the existing literature. Moreover, they are no more problematic than any attempt to simplify something as complex and stochastic as judicial role orientation. As that judge went on to say, "Precedent is obviously important, but there is also a place for public policy, justice and common sense, as well as a bit of pragmatism." Wrote another, "The short answer to most [questions] is 'it depends.' The fact is, most cases these days involve questions of statutory interpretation...with substantial caselaw fleshing them out...Judges' diverse experiences as lawyers, trial judges, etc., plus personal views on the proper role of courts, etc., have a *limited* impact on *some* cases (emphasis in original)."

Why is this examination important? Because state high court judges wield tremendous power in our legal system. In 2010, 81,439 cases were filed in state high courts. Moreover, as the final arbiters of matters under state law, these judges have broad discretion in reaching their legal conclusions. As a judge wrote in the comment section of their survey, "I believe that judges should have wide discretion to fill in the grey areas. I also know judges who base their decisions on 'an agenda.' Whether they are plaintiff or defendant driven, it doesn't matter—BOTH ARE WRONG—they are not good judges. Judges should be problem solvers—not people who create more problems!! (emphasis in original)."

## Appendix

The models of the determinants of judges' role orientations presented in this chapter could be specified in several alternative ways. This Appendix provides these alternative specifications. First, Table 4.3 reports the results of an ordered logistic regression with the 'activism' score recoded into three equally sized categories, such that an 'activism' score of $-9$, $-8$, $-7$, $-6$, and $-5$ was coded as $-1$, an 'activism' score of $-4$ and $-3$ was coded as a 0, and an 'activism' score of $-2$, $-1$, 0, 1, and 2 was coded as 1. Second, Table 4.4 reports the results of a logistic regression when the 'activism' score was dichotomized so that judges who were on the positive side

**Table 4.3** Ordered logistic regression of 'activism' score cutoffs

| Variable | Institutional model | Background model | Combined model |
|---|---|---|---|
| Institutional structure | | | |
| Judge must stand for reelection/retention election | 0.690 | | 1.302* |
| | (0.536) | | (0.763) |
| Judge must be reappointed by governor or legislature | 1.010 | | 1.279 |
| | (0.769) | | (1.100) |
| Court's professionalism score | −1.977 | | −4.026*** |
| (Salary, Docket score, and Staff) | (1.367) | | (1.416) |
| Judge's background | | | |
| Judge's ideological score | | −0.576** | −0.772*** |
| | | (0.249) | (0.238) |
| Judge's religiousness | | 0.220 | 0.258* |
| | | (0.139) | (0.144) |
| Years of service in prosecutor's office | | 0.062 | 0.095** |
| | | (0.043) | (0.038) |
| Years of service in public defender's office | | −0.113 | −0.083 |
| | | (0.073) | (0.077) |
| Experience as trial court judge | | 0.570 | 0.845** |
| | | (0.401) | (0.386) |
| Model diagnostics | | | |
| Number of observations | 120 | 112 | 112 |
| Wald chi$^2$ | 4.060 | 16.300 | 25.330 |
| Probability > chi$^2$ | 0.255 | 0.006 | 0.001 |
| McKelvey and Zavoina's R$^2$ | 0.045 | 0.151 | 0.268 |

*Note* 'Activism' score includes three equally sized categories, such that an 'activism' score of −9, −8, −7, −6, and −5 was coded as −1, an 'activism' score of −4 and −3 was coded as a 0, and an 'activism' score of −2, −1, 0, 1, and 2 was coded as 1. Numbers in parentheses are robust standard errors clustered on state. $^*p < 0.1$, $^{**}p < 0.05$, $^{***}p < 0.01$

of the 'activism' spectrum were coded as 1 and judges who were on the 'restraint' side of the 'activism' spectrum were coded as 0. In addition to these alternative dependent variable specifications, Tables 4.5, 4.6, and 4.7 test models using alternative versions of Squire's (2008) Professionalism Score variable. Finally, Table 4.8, provides an alternative specification of judicial role orientation models with the *religiousness* variable dropped to control for any possible effects that missing values for that variable might exert.

**Table 4.4** Logistic regression of dichotomized 'activism' score

| Variable | Institutional model | Background model | Combined model |
|---|---|---|---|
| Institutional structure | | | |
| Judge must stand for reelection/retention election | | | |
| Judge must be reappointed by governor or legislature | | | |
| Court's professionalism score | 1.345 | | 1.284 |
| (Salary, Docket score, and Staff) | (2.549) | | (2.204) |
| Judge's background | | | |
| Judge's ideological score | | 0.305 | 0.222 |
| | | (0.602) | (0.601) |
| Judge's religiousness | | 0.262 | 0.362 |
| | | (0.247) | (0.295) |
| Years of service in prosecutor's office | | −0.066 | −0.094 |
| | | (0.121) | (0.146) |
| Years of service in public defender's office | | | |
| Experience as trial court judge | | 0.392 | 0.738 |
| | | (0.945) | (0.978) |
| Model diagnostics | | | |
| Number of observations | 92 | 105 | 81 |
| Wald $chi^2$ | 0.280 | 4.410 | 5.560 |
| Probability > $chi^2$ | 0.598 | 0.354 | 0.351 |
| McKelvey and Zavoina's $R^2$ | 0.014 | 0.063 | 0.134 |

*Note* 'Activism' score is dichotomized so that judges who were on the positive side of the 'activism' spectrum were coded as 1 and judges who were on the 'restraint' side of the 'activism' spectrum were coded as 0. Numbers in parentheses are robust standard errors clustered on state. *$p < 0.1$, **$p < 0.05$, ***$p < 0.01$. The *popularControl*, *reappointed*, and *yrsPubDefOff* variables were dropped from the analysis as they perfectly predicted 'restraintist' judges

**Table 4.5** Ordered logistic regression of 'activism' score using Squire's second professionalism score

| Variable | Institutional model | Background model | Combined model |
|---|---|---|---|
| Institutional structure | | | |
| Judge must stand for reelection/retention election | 1.115*** | | 1.711*** |
| | (0.362) | | (0.483) |
| Judge must be reappointed by governor or legislature | 1.072 | | 1.242 |
| | (0.676) | | (0.819) |
| Court's professionalism score | −0.929 | | −2.501** |
| (Salary Premium, Docket score, and Staff) | (1.094) | | (1.233) |
| Judge's background | | | |
| Judge's ideological score | | −0.510** | −0.701*** |
| | | (0.217) | (0.209) |
| Judge's religiousness | | 0.126 | 0.169 |
| | | (0.121) | (0.123) |
| Years of service in prosecutor's office | | 0.051 | 0.059* |
| | | (0.036) | (0.033) |
| Years of service in public defender's office | | −0.231*** | −0.202** |
| | | (0.085) | (0.087) |
| Experience as trial court judge | | 0.540 | 0.797** |
| | | (0.350) | (0.347) |
| Model diagnostics | | | |
| Number of observations | 120 | 112 | 112 |
| Wald $chi^2$ | 10.070 | 22.230 | 40.200 |
| Probability > $chi^2$ | 0.018 | 0.001 | 0.000 |
| McKelvey and Zavoina's $R^2$ | 0.032 | 0.148 | 0.227 |

*Note* Numbers in parentheses are robust standard errors clustered on state. $^*p < 0.1$, $^{**}p < 0.05$, $^{***}p < 0.01$

**Table 4.6** Ordered logistic regression of 'activism' score using Squire's third professionalism score

| Variable | Institutional model | Background model | Combined model |
|---|---|---|---|
| Institutional structure | | | |
| Judge must stand for reelection/retention election | 1.106*** | | 1.701*** |
| | (0.360) | | (0.502) |
| Judge must be reappointed by governor or legislature | 1.100* | | 1.290* |
| | (0.635) | | (0.781) |
| Court's professionalism score | −1.341 | | −2.017** |
| (Salary, Discretionary Score, and Staff) | (0.993) | | (0.951) |
| Judge's background | | | |
| Judge's ideological score | | −0.510** | −0.664*** |
| | | (0.217) | (0.205) |
| Judge's religiousness | | 0.126 | 0.156 |
| | | (0.121) | (0.126) |
| Years of service in prosecutor's office | | 0.051 | 0.056* |
| | | (0.036) | (0.034) |
| Years of service in public defender's office | | −0.231*** | −0.201** |
| | | (0.085) | (0.085) |
| Experience as trial court judge | | 0.540 | 0.786** |
| | | (0.350) | (0.342) |
| Model diagnostics | | | |
| Number of observations | 120 | 112 | 112 |
| Wald $chi^2$ | 10.600 | 22.230 | 41.240 |
| Probability > $chi^2$ | 0.014 | 0.001 | 0.000 |
| McKelvey and Zavoina's $R^2$ | 0.044 | 0.148 | 0.229 |

*Note* Numbers in parentheses are robust standard errors clustered on state. $^{*}p < 0.1$, $^{**}p < 0.05$, $^{***}p < 0.01$

**Table 4.7** Ordered logistic regression of 'activism' score using Squire's fourth professionalism score

| Variable | Institutional model | Background model | Combined model |
|---|---|---|---|
| Institutional structure | | | |
| Judge must stand for reelection/retention election | 1.130*** | | 1.747*** |
| | (0.370) | | (0.511) |
| Judge must be reappointed by governor or legislature | 1.095* | | 1.298* |
| | (0.664) | | (0.798) |
| Court's professionalism score | −0.878 | | −1.733 |
| (Salary Premium, Discretionary Score, and Staff) | (1.038) | | (1.070) |
| Judge's background | | | |
| Judge's ideological score | | −0.510** | −0.682*** |
| | | (0.217) | (0.209) |
| Judge's religiousness | | 0.126 | 0.155 |
| | | (0.121) | (0.126) |
| Years of service in prosecutor's office | | 0.051 | 0.053 |
| | | (0.036) | (0.034) |
| Years of service in public defender's office | | −0.231*** | −0.200** |
| | | (0.085) | (0.085) |
| Experience as trial court judge | | 0.540 | 0.770** |
| | | (0.350) | (0.344) |
| Model diagnostics | | | |
| Number of observations | 120 | 112 | 112 |
| Wald $chi^2$ | 9.640 | 22.230 | 34.860 |
| Probability > $chi^2$ | 0.022 | 0.001 | 0.000 |
| McKelvey and Zavoina's $R^2$ | 0.033 | 0.148 | 0.220 |

*Note* Numbers in parentheses are robust standard errors clustered on state. *$p < 0.1$, **$p < 0.05$, ***$p < 0.01$

**Table 4.8** Ordered logistic regression of 'activism' score excluding judges' religiousness

| Variable | Institutional model | Background model | Combined model |
|---|---|---|---|
| Institutional structure | | | |
| Judge must stand for reelection/retention election | 1.073*** | | 1.578*** |
| | (0.341) | | (0.392) |
| Judge must be reappointed by governor or legislature | 1.062* | | 1.150* |
| | (0.642) | | (0.699) |
| Court's professionalism score | −1.612 | | −2.746*** |
| (Salary, Docket score, and Staff) | (1.140) | | (1.066) |
| Judge's background | | | |
| Judge's ideological score | | −0.605*** | −0.789*** |
| | | (0.195) | (0.182) |
| Years of service in prosecutor's office | | 0.059* | 0.070** |
| | | (0.035) | (0.033) |
| Years of service in public defender's office | | −0.197*** | −0.172*** |
| | | (0.076) | (0.065) |
| Experience as trial court judge | | 0.499 | 0.771** |
| | | (0.324) | (0.320) |
| Model diagnostics | | | |
| Number of observations | 120 | 118 | 118 |
| Wald $chi^2$ | 11.860 | 26.610 | 53.900 |
| Probability > $chi^2$ | 0.008 | 0.000 | 0.000 |
| McKelvey and Zavoina's $R^2$ | 0.045 | 0.131 | 0.213 |

*Note* Numbers in parentheses are robust standard errors clustered on state. $^{*}p < 0.1$, $^{**}p < 0.05$, $^{***}p < 0.01$

## References

Allen, I. Elaine, and Christopher A. Seaman. 2007. "Likert Scales and Data Analyses." *Quality Progress* 40(7): 64–65.
American Judicature Society. N.d. "Methods of Judicial Selection." http://www.judicialselection.us/judicial_selection/methods/selection_of_judges.cfm (April 4, 2013).
American National Election Studies. 2012. "ANES 2008 Time Series Study." February 17. http://www.electionstudies.org/studypages/2008prepost/2008prepost.htm (June 5, 2012).
Baum, Lawrence. 1994. "What Judges Want: Judges' Goals and Judicial Behavior." *Political Research Quarterly* 47(3): 749–768.
Baum, Lawrence. 1997. *The Puzzle of Judicial Behavior*. Ann Arbor: University of Michigan Press.
Berry, William D., Evan J. Ringquist, Richard C. Fording, and Russell L. Hanson. 1998. "Measuring Citizen and Government Ideology in the American States, 1960-93." *American Journal of Political Science* 42(1): 327–348.
Blake, William. 2012. "God Save This Honorable Court: Religion as a Source of Judicial Policy Preferences." *Political Research Quarterly* 65(4): 814–826.
Bonica, Adam, and Michael J. Woodruff. 2012. "State Supreme Court Ideology and "New Style" Judicial Campaigns." Stanford University. Typescript.
Bonneau, Chris W., and Melinda Gann Hall. 2009. *In Defense of Judicial Elections*. New York: Routledge.
Brace, Paul, and Brent D. Boyea. 2007. "Judicial Selection Methods and Capital Punishment in the American States." In *Running for Judge: The Rising Political, Financial, and Legal Stakes of Judicial Elections*, ed. Matthew J. Streb. New York: New York University Press.
Brace, Paul, and Melinda Gann Hall. 1990. "Neo-Institutionalism and Dissent in State Supreme Courts." *Journal of Politics* 52(1): 54–70.
Brace, Paul, and Melinda Gann Hall. 1995. "Studying Courts Comparatively: The View from the American States." *Political Research Quarterly* 48(1): 5–29.
Brace, Paul, and Melinda Gann Hall. 1997. "The Interplay of Preferences, Case Facts, Context, and Rules in the Politics of Judicial Choice." *Journal of Politics* 59(4): 1206–1231.
Brace, Paul, Laura Langer, and Melinda Gann Hall. 2000. "Measuring the Preferences of State Supreme Court Judges." *Journal of Politics* 62(2): 387–413.
Brace, Paul, Melinda Gann Hall, and Laura Langer. 2001. "Placing State Supreme Courts in State Politics." *State Politics and Policy Quarterly* 1(1): 81–108.
Choi, Stephen J., G. Mitu Gulati, and Eric A. Posner. 2007. "Professionals or Politicians: The Uncertain Empirical Case for an Elected Rather than Appointed Judiciary." University of Chicago. Typescript.
Choi, Stephen J., Mitu Gulati, and Eric A. Posner. 2009. "Judicial Evaluations and Information Forcing: Ranking State High Courts and Their Judges." *Duke Law Journal* 58: 1313–1381.
Clark, James W., and Lyndon E. Dawson. 1996. "Personal Religiousness and Ethical Judgements: An Empirical Analysis." *Journal of Business Ethics* 15(3): 359–372.
De George, Richard T. 1986. "Theological Ethics and Business Ethics." *Journal of Business Ethics* 5(6): 421–432.
Deutsch, Jan G. 1968. "Neutrality, Legitimacy, and the Supreme Court: Some Intersections Between Law and Political Science." *Stanford Law Review* 20(2): 169–261.
Flango, Victor Eugene, Lettie McSpadden Wenner, and Manfred W. Wenner. 1975. "The Concept of Judicial Role: A Methodological Note." *American Journal of Political Science* 19(2): 277–289.
Gibson, James L. 1978. "Judges' Role Orientations, Attitudes, and Decisions: An Interactive Model." *American Political Science Review* 72(3): 911–924.
Gibson, James L. 1981. "The Role Concept in Judicial Research." *Law & Policy* 3(3): 291–311.
Gibson, James L. 1983. "From Simplicity to Complexity: The Development of Theory in the Study of Judicial Behavior." *Political Behavior* 5(1): 7–49.
Glick, Henry Robert, and Kenneth N. Vines. 1969. "Law-Making in the State Judiciary: A Comparative Study of the Judicial Role in Four States." *Polity* 2(2): 142–159.

Gryski, Gerard S., and Eleanor C. Main. 1986. "Social Backgrounds as Predictors of Votes on State Courts of Last Resort: The Case of Sex Discrimination." *Western Political Quarterly* 39(3): 528–537.
Hagle, Timothy M., and Glenn E. Mitchell, II. 1992. "Goodness–of–Fit Measures for Probit and Logit." *American Journal of Political Science* 36(3): 762–784.
Hall, Melinda Gann. 1987. "Constituent Influence in State Supreme Courts: Conceptual Notes and a Case Study." *Journal of Politics* 49(4): 1117–1124.
Hall, Melinda Gann. 1992. "Electoral Politics and Strategic Voting in State Supreme Courts." *Journal of Politics* 54(2): 427–446.
Hall, Melinda Gann. 1995. "Justices as Representatives: Elections and Judicial Politics in the American States." *American Politics Research* 23(4): 485–503.
Hall, Melinda Gann. 2007. "Competition as Accountability in State Supreme Court Elections." In *Running for Judge: The Rising Political, Financial, and Legal Stakes of Judicial Elections*, ed. Matthew J. Streb. New York: New York University Press.
Hall, Melinda Gann, and Paul Brace. 1994. "The Vicissitudes of Death by Decree: Forces Influencing Capital Punishment Decision Making in State Supreme Courts." *Social Science Quarterly* 75(1): 136–151.
Hamilton, Lawrence C. 1992. *Regression with Graphics: A Second Course in Applied Statistics*. Pacific Grove: Brooks/Cole Publishing.
Hewitt, John P. 2007. *Self and Society: A Symbolic Interactionist Social Psychology*. 10th ed. Boston: Allyn and Bacon.
Howard, Jr., J. Woodford. 1977. "Role Perceptions and Behavior in Three U.S. Courts of Appeals." *Journal of Politics* 39(4): 916–938.
Howard, Robert M., and Jeffrey A. Segal. 2004. "A Preference for Deference? The Supreme Court and Judicial Review." *Political Research Quarterly* 57(1): 131–143.
Knight, Jack. 1992. *Institutions and Social Conflict*. Cambridge: Cambridge University Press.
Langer, Laura. 2003. "Strategic Considerations and Judicial Review: The Case of Workers' Compensation Laws in the American States." *Public Choice* 116(1/2): 55–78.
Leslie, Larry R. 1972. "Are High Response Rates Essential to Valid Surveys?" *Social Science Research* 1(3): 323–334.
Levin, Mark R. 2005. *Men in Black: How the Supreme Court Is Destroying America*. Washington, DC: Regnery.
Likert, Rensis. 1932. "A Technique for the Measurement of Attitudes." *Archives of Psychology* 22: 5–55.
Long, J. Scott. 1997. *Regression Models for Categorical and Limited Dependent Variables*. Thousand Oaks: Sage Publications.
Long, J. Scott, and Jeremy Freese. 2006. *Regression Models for Categorical Dependent Variables Using Stata*. 2nd ed. College Station: Stata Press Publication.
McKelvey, Richard D., and William Zavoina. 1975. "A Statistical Model for the Analysis of Ordinal Level Dependent Variables." *Journal of Mathematical Sociology* 4(1): 103–120.
Nagel, Stuart S. 1961. "Political Party Affiliation and Judges' Decisions." *American Political Science Review* 55(4): 843–850.
North, Douglass C. 1990. *Institutions, Institutional Change and Economic Performance*. Cambridge: Cambridge University Press.
Nunn, Kenneth B. 1995. "The Trial as Text: Allegory, Myth and Symbol in the Adversarial Criminal Process - A Critique of the Role of the Public Defender and a Proposal for Reform." *American Criminal Law Review* 32(3): 743–822.
Powers, Daniel A., and Yu Xie. 2000. *Statistical Models for Categorical Data Analysis*. San Diego: Academic Press.
Preiss, Jack J., and Howard J. Ehrlich. 1966. *An Examination of Role Theory: The Case of the State Police*. Lincoln: University of Nebraska Press.
Scheb, II, John M., and Thomas D. Ungs. 1987. "Competing Orientations to the Judicial Role: The Case of Tennessee Judges." *Tennessee Law Review* 54(Spring): 391–411.

Scheb, II, John M., Thomas D. Ungs, and Allison L. Hayes. 1989. "Judicial Role Orientations, Attitudes and Decision Making: A Research Note." *Western Political Quarterly* 42(3): 427–435.

Songer, Donald R., and Susan J. Tabrizi. 1999. "The Religious Right in Court: The Decision Making of Christian Evangelicals in State Supreme Courts." *Journal of Politics* 61(2): 507–526.

Squire, Peverill. 1992. "Legislative Professionalism and Membership Diversity in State Legislature." *Legislative Studies Quarterly* 17(1): 69–79.

Squire, Peverill. 2007. "Measuring Legislative Professionalism: The Squire Index Revisited." *State Politics and Policy Quarterly* 7(2): 211–227.

Squire, Peverill. 2008. "Measuring the Professionalization of U. S. State Courts of Last Resort." *State Politics & Policy Quarterly* 8(3): 223–238.

Streb, Matthew J., ed. 2007. *Running for Judge: The Rising Political, Financial, and Legal Stakes of Judicial Elections*. New York: New York University Press.

Ulmer, S. Sidney. 1973. "Social Background as an Indicator to the Votes of Supreme Court Justices in Criminal Cases: 1947-1956 Terms." *American Journal of Political Science* 17(3): 622–630.

Vaidik, Nancy. 2011. "Three Views from the Bench." In *What's Law Got to Do with It? What Judges Do, Why They Do It, and What's at Stake*, ed. Charles Gardner Geyh. Stanford: Stanford University Press.

Windmeijer, Frank A. G. 1995. "Goodness–of–Fit Measures in binary choice models." *Econometric Reviews* 14(1): 101–116.

Wold, John T. 1974. "Political Orientations, Social Backgrounds, and Role Perceptions of State Supreme Court Judges." *Western Political Quarterly* 27(2): 239–248.

Wold, John T., and John H. Culver. 1987. "The Defeat of the California Justices: The Campaign, the Electorate, and the Issue of Judicial Accountability." *Judicature* 70(6): 348–355.

Yarnold, Barbara M. 2000. "Did Circuit Courts of Appeals Judges Overcome Their Own Religions in Cases Involving Religious Liberties? 1970-1990." *Review of Religious Research* 42(1): 79–86.

# Chapter 5
# The Impact of the Judicial Role Orientation

In a speech entitled "The Role of the Judge in the Twenty-First Century," U.S. Court of Appeals Judge Richard Posner (2006, 1055) argues that "American appellate judges are constrained legislators." Controversially, he rejects the view "that judges legislate only after they have tried and failed to decide the case by reference to the orthodox legal materials of (mainly) text and precedent," or what he calls playing the game (2006, 1055). Rather, he says, "They start by making the 'legislative' judgment as to what decision would have good consequences—would be, in other words, good policy—and then see whether that judgment is blocked by the orthodox materials" (2006, 1055). He continues,

> But I have yet to confront the really difficult question. For even wholehearted compliance with the rules of the game leaves appellate judges with broad discretion in many cases. The question is what determines the judge's discretionary judgment. The fact that he's going to have to make a legislative determination, though with awareness that his legislative scope differs from that of the official legislators (narrower in some respects but broader in others), does not tell him or us what determination among the possible choices he's going to make. Within the discretionary zone, moreover, the judge's twin objectives of improving the world and playing the judicial game merge. But it is not a happy merger; rather it is a marriage of convenience, because the rule that permits (or maybe commands) the judge to legislate in the open area makes an uneasy fit with the other rules of the game, which seek to distinguish the judicial from the legislative role... (2006, 1058)

One potential determinant of a judge's exercise of his or her discretion is the judge's role orientation. Yet, while much has been written about the judicial role orientation,[1] researchers have yet to examine, in a comprehensive manner, what effect judicial role orientation has on judicial behavior. However, as Jewell (1970, 486) writes about the legislative role orientation, "A specific role orientation means a predisposition or inclination to act in a particular way; it indicates a probability, not a certainty, about voting or any other action. If we know enough about a legislator's role concepts, we should be able to predict more accurately how he will respond to demands, how he will vote." This chapter begins, in Sect. 5.1, by discussing the link

[1] For a review of the existing literature on the role orientation of state high court judges, see Chap. 2.



R.V. Carman, Jr., *Making Good Law or Good Policy?*,
DOI 10.1007/978-3-319-53381-0_5

between the judicial role orientation and judicial behavior. An empirical investigation of the effect judicial role orientation has on judicial decision–making is devised in Sect. 5.2, the results of which are discussed in Sect. 5.3.

## 5.1 Role Orientation and Role Behavior

Role theory, a school of thought based in social psychology, consists of "a particular viewpoint regarding those facts presumed to be influential in governing human behavior" (Thomas and Biddle 1966, 4).[2] Drawing from the analogy of a theatrical actor in a stage play, role theorists argue "that performance results from the social prescriptions and behavior of others, and that individual variations in performance, to the extent that they do occur, are expressed within the framework created by these factors" (Thomas and Biddle 1966, 4). Therefore, role theory is premised on the core belief that an individual's role orientation (the product of synthesizing institutional rules, one's own preconceived idea of the proper role orientation, and the role expectations of others) will affect that individual's behavior (Biddle 1986).

Beyond this theoretical expectation, those studies that examine the judicial role orientation report role orientation's effect on judicial behavior. For example, James (1968) explores the role orientations of U.S. Supreme Court Justices Robert H. Jackson and William O. Douglas. She finds that their role orientations led the former to place greater emphasis on stability and continuity in the law,[3] and led the latter to value adaptability and flexibility in the law.[4] This work is certainly limited by its use of inductive, rather than deductive reasoning,[5] and its focus on just two justices, but it provided early support for the contention that role orientation affects behavior.

Also exploring the effect that role orientation has on the behavior of federal judges, Howard (1977) examines judges on the U.S. Courts of Appeal for the Second, Fifth, and D.C. Circuits. Using the judges' votes in particular issue areas as the dependent variable,[6] and the judges' role orientation and their self–reported pre–court ideology as independent variables, he finds that the judges' role orientations are better predictors of case outcomes than are the judges' pre–judicial political outlooks.

In the realm of state courts, Becker (1966) examines the role orientation of 22 Hawaiian judges. He finds that judges who consider precedent to be the most important decisional factor are more likely to rule, as Becker (1966) refers to it,

---

[2]For a chronicling of the development of role theory and a fuller explanation of the judicial role orientation, see Chaps. 2 and 4.

[3]A role orientation that is referred to in this work as that of 'restraintist.'

[4]A role orientation that is referred to in this work as that of 'activist.'

[5]James (1968) uses inductive reasoning because she uses the writings of these justices to infer their role orientation.

[6]The issue areas Howard (1977) examines are: employee injury claims, other personal injury claims, patent and copyright cases, labor/management disputes, income tax challenges, civil rights suits, prisoner petitions, and criminal cases.

'objectively.' Jaros and Mendelsohn (1967) explore the effect role orientation has on traffic court sentencing.[7] These authors conclude that, in low to moderately severe crimes, defendants who dress poorly (and therefore do not show the 'proper' deference to the role rights granted to judges) are more likely to be jailed than are defendants who dress well (and therefore show the 'proper' deference to the role rights granted to judges).[8]

Gibson (1977) studies the severity of the sentences imposed by the judges of the Superior Court of Fulton County, Georgia. He finds that, for five of the 11 judges studied, seven non–legal stimuli explained 20% or more of the variance in sentencing behavior, leading Gibson (1977, 999) to conclude that "activism…[is] the ability of political or non–legal factors to explain variation in voting behavior." Gibson (1978) examines the effect both ideology and role orientation have on Iowa trial court judges by reviewing their sentencing behavior. Gibson (1978) finds that judges' role orientations appear to intervene between ideology and sentence.

Finally, Scheb et al. (1991) test Gibson's (1978) model that judges' behavior derives from their attitudes, role orientation, and the interaction of both. To test this theory, they surveyed 151 state high court judges to identify the judges' role orientations and their ideology. Scheb et al. (1991) use this information to predict the judges' support for the prosecution. The authors find, contrary to Gibson's (1978) expectation, that judicial role orientation is independent of ideology and that role orientation and behavior are directly related.

Of these studies, only Scheb et al. (1991) attempt to comprehensively examine the effect that judicial role orientation has on the judges' behavior: Becker (1966) studies only 22 Hawaiian judges; Jaros and Mendelsohn (1967) looks only at judges of the Detroit Traffic Court; Gibson (1977) explores only Superior Court judges in Fulton County Georgia; and Gibson (1978) investigates only Iowa trial court judges. Despite the laudable breadth of the study, Scheb et al.'s (1991) use of support for the prosecution as their measure of judicial behavior is problematic because their operationalization of the judicial role orientation does not measure support for the prosecution.

## 5.2 Research Design

Role theory leads to the expectation that an individual's role orientation, which was conceptualized in Chap. 2 as his or her view about the limits of proper behavior, affects his or her behavior. In the field of judicial politics, as chronicled above, there exists some empirical support for the expectation that judges' role orientations

[7]Unfortunately, as Gibson (1981b) explains, like James (1968), the observed decisional behavior of the judges is used to infer the existence of particular role orientations.

[8]As Jaros and Mendelsohn (1967, 476) explain, "Role are characterized not only by *obligations* but also by *rights*. The judge is expected to perform certain behaviors as a consequence of his position, but because of his position he may expect that others will exhibit certain kinds of behavior toward him."

affect their behavior. This is important because, practically speaking, judges' role orientations only matter to the extent that they affect judges' behavior. In order to test this theory, an empirical study of state high court judges was designed.

There exists much literature on judicial review in the states. However the literature does not speak to the effect that a state high court judge's role orientation has on his or her votes in such cases. For example, Emmert (1992) constructs an integrated model of state high court judicial decision–making in cases involving challenges to the constitutionality of state laws. The first component of the integrated model is "The Issues Model." This model supposes that state high court judges are more likely to strike down cases dealing with a particular issue than cases dealing with other issues. The issue areas Emmert (1992) includes are: criminal cases,[9] economic regulation cases,[10] private cases,[11] civil liberties cases,[12] and government and political cases.[13]

The second component of Emmert's (1992) integrated model is "The Party Capability Model." Here, building on Galanter (1974), Emmert (1992) expects that "organizational litigants are more successful in the judicial arena than are individuals because they possess superior political and economic resources, because they can obtain better legal talent, and because they have more experience in using the legal system" (1992, 546). The third component of his integrated model is "The Constitutional Grounds Model." Here, borrowing from Tarr and Porter (1988), Emmert (1992, 547) hypothesizes that, because "[t]he detailed, complex nature of state constitutions provides potential litigants with numerous grounds on which to challenge state laws and gives courts multiple bases on which to rely in declaring laws unconstitutional," the more detailed the state constitution is, "the greater the likelihood of participation by the state supreme court in determining the ultimate policy in the state" (Tarr and Porter 1988, 50–51).

The forth component of Emmert's (1992) integrated model is "The Centrality Model." In this model, Emmert (1992) attempts to control for what essentially amounts to frivolous constitutional claims brought by litigants. He expects that "as the number of issues raised in the case increases, the probability of the challenged statute being overturned would decrease" (1992, 548). The final component of his integrated model is "The Lower Court Ruling Model." Here, Emmert (1992, 548) adopts an approach similar to Segal (1984) by controlling for the fact that "state supreme courts affirm more than 60% of the lower court decisions that they review" because "[w]hile trial court and intermediate appellate court judges may not always agree with state supreme court justices on controversial questions of policy, they

[9]Criminal cases are those that involved constitutional challenges to "laws defining crimes, prescribing penalties, or governing trial procedure" (Emmert 1992, 544–545).

[10]Economic regulation cases are were those that involved constitutional challenges to "policies that govern the use and distribution of economic resources" (Emmert 1992, 545).

[11]Private cases are those that involved constitutional challenges to "statutes of limitations, medical malpractice statutes,…[and] family law statutes…" (Emmert 1992, 545).

[12]Civil liberties cases are those that involved constitutional challenges to "class–based discrimination, fundamental freedoms, and victimless crimes" (Emmert 1992, 545).

[13]Government and political cases are those that involved "disputes among government officials regarding authority and jurisdiction" (Emmert 1992, 546).

are probably just as able to identify patently unmeritorious constitutional claims." Emmert (1992, 548) expects that "when a lower court rules that a law violates the state or federal constitution, the state supreme court will be more likely to overturn the statute in question."

Emmert (1992) finds compelling support for his integrated model. Civil liberties and government/political cases are more likely to be overturned, while challenges in criminal cases are less likely to be successful. Challenges to a law based on state grounds alone are more successful than challenges that include state and federal or no specific grounds. The greater the number of issues raised by the challenge, the less likely the challenge is to be successful. Finally, challenged laws struck down by the lower court are likely to be successful on appeal.

Next, Emmert and Traut (1992) test the theory that "state high courts frequently interpret state constitutional provisions in ways that provide greater protection for individual rights than does the U.S. Constitution as interpreted by the U.S. Supreme Court," a theory termed "New Judicial Federalism" by Porter (1982). To do so, they construct a dataset of all cases involving constitutional challenges to state laws decided by the state high courts between 1981 and 1985. The authors find that state high courts are more likely to strike down laws as unconstitutional when the challenge is made on state constitutional grounds. They reason this may either be because: (1) the judges prefer using their own state constitution rather than the U.S. Constitution since they know that decisions that rest solely on state grounds cannot later be reversed by the U.S. Supreme Court, or (2) state constitutions may provide more avenues for judicial policymaking.

To date, one of the important works on this topic is Langer's *Judicial Review in State Supreme Courts: A Comparative Study*. Langer (2002) argues that judicial votes to both review and invalidate state laws are influenced by the anticipated reaction from the governor and the legislature. "Fundamentally, judges do not operate in a vacuum. Rather state supreme court justices are expected to alter their votes in response to the anticipated reactions from the legislature and governor" (2002, 16). Said another way, under some conditions state high court judges *can* vote sincerely and strike down laws with which they disagree. Under other conditions state high court judges *must* act strategically and instead uphold laws with which they disagree for fear of retaliation.

To construct a theory to explain when state high court judges can act sincerely and when they must act strategically, building on the seminal works of Murphy (1964) and Rohde and Spaeth (1976), Langer (2002, 39) first assumes state high court judges are "rational acts who pursue at least two goals: (1) translating their sincere preferences in public policy, and (2) retaining their seat on the bench." Her next key assumption is that "when state justices exercise their power of judicial review, they knowingly risk electoral or policy retaliation for their actions" (2002, 40). The third and final key assumption is that "justices have some information regarding the preferences of the legislature and governor" and that "state government is expected to incur costs when government retaliates against a judge for his/her decisions" (2002, 40).

These assumptions lead Langer (2002) to the following theory: There exists a range of policy decisions that are acceptable to the governor and the legislature because the cost incurred to them to fight these decisions is too high. Judges are free to act sincerely when their decision lies within this 'safety zone.' Judges whose policy preferences lie outside of this 'safety zone' must act strategically, else they will face retaliation. Langer (2002) tests this theory by examining decisions in all fifty states from 1970–1993 in four issue areas of varying salience to the political branches: election and campaign legislation, workers' compensation legislation, unemployment compensation legislation, and welfare legislation. She finds support for her safety zone theory in three of the four issue areas.

Finally, following up on her earlier piece, Langer (2003) examines judicial review decisions in workers' compensation claims decided by state high court judges from 1970–1993. She contends, as she did in her previous work, that in some situations judges can act sincerely while in other situations they must act strategically. Langer (2003) finds, not surprisingly, that judges' ideologies influence their decision–making. However, a judge's use of ideology is conditional upon (1) the ideological distance between the judge and other relevant actors, and (2) the institutional rules under which the judge is operating. These facts matter because they affect whether the political branches (1) have the need to retaliate against judges, and (2) have the ability to retaliate against judges. "For example, absent rules that afford retaliatory mechanisms to the chief justice, justices do not alter their behavior according to the preferences of the chief justice… On the other hand, judges reference the ideology of the chief justice when the chief justice controls opinion assignment" (2003, 70).

Similarly, the preferences of amici participants influence the likelihood that a judge will vote to strike down a workers' compensation law. However, Langer (2003) finds, their impact on judges' decisions is conditioned by the state's judicial retention procedures. State high court judges that are not retained in popular elections are significantly more likely to invalidate a workers' compensation statute when amicus curiae briefs were filed on behalf of the injured worker. On the other hand, elected state high court judges are significantly less likely to entertain the preferences of the amici participants. "These results imply that justices in states where their electoral fate is not tied directly to the citizenry exhibit less concern for majoritarian preferences" (2003, 70).

Retaliation mechanisms available to the governor, legislature, and the chief justice curtail judges' votes to invalidate state laws in those instances when institutional rules create or enhance sanctions. "For example, justices dependent upon the legislature or governor for retention were significantly less likely to invalidate laws. Electoral insularity from these actors seemingly encourages judges to impute their preferences on issues of public policy" (2003, 72).

None of these authors consider, however, the effect judges' role orientations have on their decisions in judicial review cases. As the judicial role orientation was operationalized in Chap. 2 as lying on the 'activist–restraintist' spectrum and one of the dimensions on which the judicial role orientation was measured was as judicial deference to the political branches of government (i.e., the executive and the legislature), an examination of cases in which state high courts were asked to consider the constitutionality of state and local laws provide an exceptionally good (and theoretically sound) test of the effect judges' role orientations have on judicial decision–making.

Moreover, there is reason to believe that constitutional cases present a fertile ground for the exercise of judicial discretion. Posner (2006, 1053) explains, "There is almost always a zone of reasonableness within which a decision either way can be defended persuasively, or at least plausibly, using the resources of judicial rhetoric. But the zone can be narrow or wide—narrow when formalist analysis provides a satisfactory solution, wide when it does not. Within the zone, a decision cannot be labeled 'right' or 'wrong'; truth just is not in the picture." The zone of reasonableness, Posner (2006, 1066) argues, "is widest in constitutional cases in which the judges' emotions are engaged, because the constitutional text provides little guidance and emotion opposes dispassionate consideration of the systemic factors that induce judges to rein in their discretion. Rather than think that judges can be bludgeoned into agreeing to adopt one of the constitutional theories to channel their discretion, we should bow to the inevitable…"

The survey that was created to obtain the judges' role orientations was deployed in the fall of 2011.[14] Therefore, in order to maximize both efficiency and validity, voting behavior in 2011 was examined. While examining additional years would certainly increase the number of cases, such endeavors would provide diminishing returns as some of the survey respondents did not join their court until in or about 2011 while yet others left their court in or about 2011. In addition, as the surveys captured the judges' role orientations at the moment he or she responded to the survey, and role orientations are subject to change (Biddle 1979), expanding the dates under consideration could negatively effect the validity of the measure.

The nature of this examination required the collection of decisional data. To collect these data, first, LexisNexis was used to select all constitutional cases decided in 2011 by state high courts that included a survey respondent. The search procedure used was: (1) "constitution!" or "unconstitution!" appearing in LexisNexis' Procedural Posture, Overview, or Outcome section; and (2) "affirmed" or "reversed" appearing in LexisNexis' Outcome section.[15] The exclamation points in the first search commands instruct LexisNexis to retrieve all forms of the search term by adding letters in place of the exclamation points (returning, for example, the words "constitutional," "constitutionality," "unconstitutional," etc.). To allow for future analyses that include the treatment of the lower court's decision, the search commands "affirmed" or "reversed" was used to limit the cases returned to only those in which the lower court's decision was resolved in a definitively positive or negative manner.

---

[14]For more information about the survey design and implementation, see Chap. 3.

[15]The exact search phrase was: "DATE AFT(12/31/2010) AND DATE BEF(01/01/2012) AND POSTURE(constitution!) OR POSTURE(unconstitution!) OR OVERVIEW(constitution!) OR OVERVIEW(unconstitution!) OR OUTCOME(constitution!) OR OUTCOME(unconstitution!) AND OUTCOME(affirmed) OR OUTCOME(reversed)."

The resulting list of cases returned by LexisNexis included 366 court cases that met this initial search criteria. Per state, the number of court cases ranged from a low of one court case to a high of 26 court cases. As to the case distribution: the mean number per state was 7.8 court cases, the median number per state was 7 court cases, and the modal number per state was 7 court cases.

Next, each court case returned by LexisNexis was checked to ensure that it should be included in the dataset. Those cases that did not include a judge who responded to the mail survey were eliminated. These came about in cases of recusal, or when a judge left the court early in the year, or joined the court late in the year. The cases that remained were read in their entirety to determine whether they met the inclusion criteria. Cases involving challenges to statutes as applied were excluded,[16] as were cases involving challenges to administrative agency rules, executive orders, rules of civil and criminal procedure, etc. For a case to be coded as resulting in a declaration on the constitutionality of a state or local law, an explicit statement to that effect in the opinion was required. Rulings of unconstitutional in part were coded as invalidations.[17]

A total of 107 court cases survived elimination. This resulting dataset includes cases from 41 of the 52 high courts. These court cases include votes of 104 unique survey respondents, which results in a total of 267 case–vote observations. Per state, the number of case–vote observations range from a low of 0 to a high of 26. The mean number per state is 6.8 case–votes, the median number per state is 5 case–votes, and the modal number per state is 4 case–votes.

The first variables that were coded were identification variables.[18,19] The first of these variables, *judgeID*, is a four–digit variable uniquely identifying each judge in the dataset. The first two numbers identify the state. The third and fourth numbers correspond with a randomly assigned identification number. The second variable, *judgeName*, is a string variable containing the judge's first and last name. The *citation* variable is a string variable identifying each case in the dataset by its regional reporter

---

[16]Cases in which the substance of a state or local law was not challenged as unconstitutional, but rather only the application of a state or local law to a party, were excluded from the dataset. This decision was made to be consistent with the dependent variable's conceptualization: judicial deference to the political branches of government. Excluding challenges to the application of a state or local law means that, if a judge disproves of a law, he or she cannot merely waive the law's application to a particular party, but must rather confront the political branch by striking down the law.

[17]A list of the cases included in this dataset, and the laws that were challenged as unconstitutional, is provided in Table 5.4 in the Appendix.

[18]See the Appendix for the codebook.

[19]To ensure the quality of variable coding, a random sample of ten cases were recoded one month later in a separate dataset. A comparison of the results showed no differences in variable coding between the dataset and the 10 case sample.

citation.[20] The string variables *petitioner* and *respondent* identify the name of the petitioner and respondent, respectively. Finally, the *decisionDate* variable provides the date the court's decision was released.

Next, case background variables were coded. The first variable, *issueArea* identifies the subject matter of the controversy. If the constitutional challenge in a case raised a civil liberty or civil right claim (excluding issues pertaining to criminal law and criminal procedure) it was coded as 1, an issue under criminal law or criminal procedure was coded as 2, a challenge of an economic activity or economic regulation was coded as 3, and cases that fell into neither of these categories was coded as 4.[21] The distribution of these cases by legal area include: 54 case–vote observations in cases raising civil rights or civil liberties claims, 119 case–vote observations in cases raising criminal law and criminal procedure issues, 68 case–vote observations in cases raising issues of economic activity or economic regulation, and 26 case–vote observations in cases not in one of the previous categories.

The next variable, the dichotomous *stateGov*, indicates whether the state government was a party to the case. The state government was a party in 184 of the 267 case–vote observations. The last two variables, the dichotomous *governmentPetitioner* and *governmentRespondent*, indicate whether the state government was listed as the case's petitioner or respondent, respectively.[22] Of the 184 case–vote observations in which the state government was a party, in 42 case–vote observations the government was the petitioner and in 142 case–vote observations the government was the respondent.

The final set of variables coded were outcome variables. The *majVotes* and *minVotes* variables indicate the number of judges in the majority and minority, respectively. The *minWinningCoalition* variable indicates whether the case was won by one vote. Six of the 267 case–vote observations were in cases where the outcome was decided by one vote. The *decisionDirection* variable indicates the ideological direction of the court's decision.[23] In all, 144 of the 267 case–vote observations were

---

[20]The regional reporter system, created by West Publishing Company, divides the country into seven geographic regions. In these volumes, the decisions of multiple state courts are published together. The regional reporters are: the Atlantic Reporter, the North Eastern Reporter, the North Western Reporter, the Pacific Reporter, the South Eastern Reporter, the Southern Reporter, and the South Western Reporter.

[21]These include: administrative law, court jurisdiction, educational funding, incorporation of local governments, and tort law.

[22]There are instances in the data where the state government was not a party to a constitutional challenge. In some of these cases, local governments were defending the constitutionality of local laws. An example that does not include any level of government is a case where a property owner sought to overturn the automatic easement granted to a utility company.

[23]The ideological variables were coded consistent with Spaeth et al. (2013). As such, for example, a liberal outcome in the area of civil liberties and civil rights or criminal law and criminal procedure include: anti–government in the context of due process rights, pro–affirmative action, pro–child or juvenile, pro–civil liberties or civil rights claimant, pro–female in abortion, pro–indigent, pro–person accused or convicted of crime, pro–privacy, or pro–underdog. A liberal outcome in the area of economic activity and economic regulation include: anti–business, anti–employer, pro–competition,

in cases where the court decided conservatively, 101 were in cases where the court decided liberally, and 22 were in cases where the ideological direction of the court's decision was indiscernible.[24]

Next, the dichotomous *declarationUncon* and *disposition* indicate whether the court declared a state or local law unconstitutional and whether the court affirmed or reversed the trial court, respectively. In 73 of the 267 case–vote observations the court struck down a state or local law as unconstitutional and in 189 of the 267 case–vote observations the court affirmed the decisions of the trial court. The judge–centered *vote* indicates whether the judge voted with the majority opinion or dissented from the majority opinion. In 251 of the 267 case–vote observations, the judge voted with the majority. Lastly, *direction* indicates the ideological direction of the judge's vote. In 156 of the 267 case–vote observations, the judge voted conservatively. In 89, he or she voted liberally. In 22, the ideological direction of the judge's vote was indiscernible.[25]

As described above, the behavior being analyzed is the survey respondent's vote in each case where a state or local law was challenged as unconstitutional decided in 2011. Some examples of laws that were challenged during this time include caps on punitive damages, a gasoline price–gouging statute, and a law requiring businesses that offer live nude entertainment and allow the consumption of alcohol on their premises to pay a tax for each customer admitted.

Summary statistics with associated expectations for each variable are presented in Table 5.1. To serve as a judge–centered dependent variable, a dichotomous *voteUncon* was created such that a 0 indicates that the judge voted to uphold the challenged state or local law and a 1 indicates that the judge voted to strike down the challenged state or local law as unconstitutional. In 61 of the 267 case–vote observations, the judge voted to strike down the challenged state or local law as unconstitutional. In 206 of the 267 case–vote observations, the judge voted to uphold the challenged law.

The model's main independent variable tests the theory that judges' role orientations affect their behavior. This variable, *activismScore*, is fully described in Chap. 4 where it serves as that chapter's dependent variable. The ordinal *activismScore* places judges on the 'activist–restraintist' spectrum. While the variable is skewed to the 'restraintist' end of the spectrum such that the modal score was −3 and the most 'activist' judge was scored +2, the data does resemble a normal distribution.[26] If

---

pro–consumer, pro–debtor, pro–environmental protection, pro–government, pro–indigent, or pro–injured person.

[24]For example, one instance in which the customary ideological coding rules provided no clear guidance was in a case where local school districts challenged a statute creating charter schools as a violation of the state constitution's "fundamental principle of exclusive local control of general primary and secondary public education."

[25]Cases in which the ideological direction of a judge's vote was indiscernible were those cases in which the ideological direction of the court's decision was indiscernible.

[26]A histogram of this variable is presented in Fig. 4.1 in Chap. 4.

**Table 5.1** Summary statistics with associated expectations

| Variable | Expectation | Mean/Mode | Std. Dev. | Range |
|---|---|---|---|---|
| **Dependent variable** | | | | |
| Judge's vote to declare law unconstitutional | N/A | 0.00 | 0.42 | 0.0–1.0 |
| **Independent variables** | | | | |
| Judge's 'Activism' score | + | −3.49 | 2.49 | −9.0–2.0 |
| Court's discretionary docket control | + | 2.00 | 0.79 | 0.0–2.0 |
| State government party to case | − | 1.00 | 0.46 | 0.0–1.0 |
| Judge's ideological score | − | −0.09 | 0.79 | −1.5–1.5 |
| Elected, non–judicial experience | + | 0.36 | 0.48 | 0.0–1.0 |

*Note* The universe of cases are those: decided in 2011 by state high court judges who responded to the mail survey discussed in Chap. 3; identified by a LexisNexis search in which the term "constitution!" or "unconstitution!" appears in LexisNexis' Procedural Posture, Overview, or Outcome section and"affirmed" or "reversed" appears in the Outcome section; and those which, after careful reading, presented a facial challenge to the constitutionality of a state or local law. See the Appendix for the codebook. Judges' 'activism' score reflect the judges' level of agreement with six 'activist' statements. For more information about this variable, see Chap. 4

judges' role orientations matter, than the more 'activist' a judge is, the more likely he or she should be to strike down a state or local law as unconstitutional.

One of the statistically significant determinants of a judge's role orientation, as discussed in Chap. 4, is a judge's ideology. To be assured that any observable effect a judge's role orientation might have on a judge's proclivity to vote to strike down a state or local law as unconstitutional is not merely a reflection of ideology, a two–stage strategy was developed. First, the two variables were compared. To do so, judges' ideological scores, discussed in Chap. 4, were collapsed such that an ideological score of −0.5 or less was coded as conservative, an ideological score between −0.5 and 0.5 was coded as moderate, and an ideological score of 0.5 or greater was coded as liberal. These ideological scores were than compared to judges' voting behavior. The results are presented in Table 5.2.

The column percentages reveal little deviation between a judge's vote to strike a state or local law as unconstitutional and his or her ideology. To be sure that there is not a statistically significant relationship between these two variables that is not discernible from the column percentages, the Pearson $\chi^2$ value was calculated. The Pearson $\chi^2$ value for the relationship between these two variables is 0.51, which indicates that there is not a statistically significant relationship between a judge's vote to declare a state or local law unconstitutional and the judge's ideology. We can therefore be confident that any statistical relationship between the judge's vote and the judge's role orientation is not merely a reflection of the judge's ideology.

Several court–, case–, and judge–specific variables were included in the model as they were expected to influence judges' votes in judicial review cases. The first of which, *discretion*, is a proxy variable to indicate the extent to which the state high

**Table 5.2** Judge's vote to strike law as unconstitutional by judge's ideology

| Vote | Judge's Ideology | | | |
|---|---|---|---|---|
| | Conservative | Moderate | Liberal | Total |
| Constitutional | 69 | 75 | 57 | 201 |
| | 79% | 75% | 76% | 77% |
| Unconstitutional | 18 | 25 | 18 | 61 |
| | 21% | 21% | 24% | 23% |
| Total | 87 | 100 | 75 | 262 |
| | 100% | 100% | 100% | 100% |

*Source* Ideology scores are Bonica and Woodruff's (2012), collapsed such that an ideological score of −0.5 is conservative, an ideological score between −0.5 and 0.5 is moderate, and an ideological score of 0.5 or greater is liberal. Vote data coded from case data available on LexisNexis
*Note* Pearson $\chi^2 = 0.51$

court has discretion over its docket. Data for this variable comes from the Bureau of Justice Statistics (2000). This variable was coded such that a state high court having no jurisdiction over sentencing appeals was coded as 0, mandatory jurisdiction over sentencing appeals was coded was 1, and discretionary jurisdiction over sentencing appeals was coded as 2.[27] In all, 58 of the 267 case–vote observations were made by judges on courts with no jurisdiction over sentencing appeals, 81 were made by judges on courts with mandatory jurisdiction over sentencing appeals, and 128 were made by judges on courts with discretionary jurisdiction over sentencing appeals.

As Tarr and Porter (1988) note, the agenda of state high courts with a discretionary docket is different than state higher courts without a discretionary docket. In states without discretionary dockets, the state high court must hear a "great many cases in which only one decision is easily justified under the law" (Baum 1994, 754). Meanwhile, judges in states with discretionary dockets are "more concerned with the content of their decisions and less with processing and disposing of cases" (Baum 1994, 752). Empirically, Eisenberg and Miller (2009) find that state high courts reverse 28.1% of cases under mandatory jurisdiction and 51.6% of cases under discretionary jurisdiction. Similarly, there are dissents in 18.8% of cases decided under

[27] The Bureau of Justice Statistics (2000) provides the extent to which state high courts have discretionary control over their docket in seven categories: civil appeals, criminal appeals, administrative agency appeals, extraordinary writs, guilty pleas, post conviction requests for relief, death penalty appeals, and sentencing appeals. No state high court has discretionary control over death penalty appeals. By far, the category of appeals in which state high courts have the greatest variation in the degree of discretion is sentencing appeals. A total of 21.7% of case–observations were decided by states without jurisdiction over sentencing appeals, 30.3% of case–observations were decided by states with mandatory jurisdiction over sentencing appeals, and 47.9% of case–observations were decided by states with discretionary jurisdiction over sentencing appeals. Therefore discretion over sentencing appeals was chosen as a proxy for the level of discretion a state high court has over its docket. A model specified with an alternative proxy variable for discretionary docket control, whether a state's judiciary includes an intermediate appellate court, is provided in Table 5.5 in Appendix.

mandatory jurisdiction and dissents in 26.7% of cases decided under discretionary jurisdiction. Therefore, the presence of a discretionary docket should increase the likelihood of a state high court judge striking down a law as unconstitutional because these judges will review fewer easy, routine, or simple cases and instead choose cases that present important controversies.[28]

Scigliano (1971), Segal (1988), McGuire (1995), Collins (2004), among others, report the "federal government's extraordinary success in the [U.S. Supreme] Court, both as party and as amicus" (Baum 1997, 52). Indeed, Galanter's (1974) theory of litigant resources argues that the federal government is the most successful party in federal cases. Since state governments involved in litigation in state courts are similarly situated to the federal government involved in litigation in federal courts, it stands to reason that this federal resource expectation should extend to the states. Yet, surprisingly, few studies of judicial review in state high courts include a variable to reflect whether the state government is a party to the case.

Therefore, borrowing from Emmert's (1992) "Party Capability Model," the model's third independent variable, *stateGov*, indicates the presence of the state government as a party to the case. The dichotomous *stateGov* was coded such that a 0 indicates that the state was not a party to the case and a 1 indicates that the state was a party to the case. Of the 107 court cases in the data, 73 include the state government as a party and 34 do not. Extending the logic from the federal level, the presence of the state government as a party to the case should make the state high court judge less likely to strike down a law as unconstitutional.

As discussed in Chap. 4, one of the statistically significant determinants of a judge's role orientation is a judge's ideology. As such, the judge's ideology must be controlled for in order to be assured that any effect observed in this chapter's model of votes in judicial review cases is not merely a reflection of his or her ideology. To do so, ideological scores developed by Bonica and Woodruff (2012) are used.[29] These scores range from −1.52 (most liberal) to 1.51 (most conservative) with a mean value of −0.09 and a standard deviation of 0.79. Following the logic of Chap. 4, if ideology does exert a statistically significant effect in judicial review cases, the more liberal a judge is, the more likely he or she should be to strike down a state or local law as unconstitutional.

"Because judges have substantial discretion in decision–making, personal experiences, values and attitudes have an impact on their decisions" (Glick and Emmert 1986, 108). Judges who have experience serving in a political position might very well behave differently than judges who do not have this experience.[30] As Baum (1997, 63) notes, "Lawyers who spend their whole pre–judicial careers in legal practice might tend to think about legal policy from a legal perspective, while those who have devoted themselves to politics and government might be more policy–oriented."

[28]For a further discussion of the role that discretionary docket control has on the selection of cases, see, for example, Tanenhaus et al. (1963) and Teger and Kosinski (1980).

[29]For more information about this variable, see Chap. 4.

[30]See, for example, Nagel (1961) and Gryski and Main (1986).

Therefore, the model's fifth independent variable indicates whether the judge reported on the survey instrument to having previously held a non–judicial elected office. The dichotomous *elctdNonJudOff* was coded such that a 0 indicates that the judge reported to not having this experience and a 1 indicates that the judge reported to having this experience. Of the 267 case–vote observations, 96 were made by judges with this experience and 171 were made without this experience. Following Baum's (1997) logic, the experience of having served in a political position should make a judge more likely to strike down a law as unconstitutional.

Finally, as Langer (2003, 66) explains, "The preferences of other actors also might curtail judicial behavior more when institutional rules governing tenure security increase the electoral vulnerability of justices. Justices operating in states where they are retained by the legislature and governor, for example, might be more responsive to the preferences of these government actors." It follows logically then that judges who are subject to reappointment by the political branches of government should be less likely to strike down laws passed by those political branches; these judges might very well lose their job for doing so.

Thus, one last variable was reasoned to be influential. The dichotomous *reappointed* was coded such that a 0 indicates that the judge was not subject to reappointment by the governor or legislature and a 1 indicates that the judge was subject to reappointment by the governor or legislature. Of the 104 judges in the data, 88 were not subject to reappointment by the governor or the legislature and 16 were. It was expected that those judges who are subject to reappointment by the governor or legislature would be most reluctant to strike down laws as unconstitutional—particularly those laws enacted by the state—for fear of losing their job. However, upon conducting statistical analyses, this variable proved to be too reliable in its explanatory power: no judge that was subject to reappointment by the political branches voted to strike down a state or local law as unconstitutional. This lack of variation necessitated estimating the model without this variable.

## 5.3 Results and Discussion

As the dependent variable, *voteUncon*, is dichotomous, a logistic regression was specified. The results of this model predicting judges' votes on the constitutionality of state and local laws based upon the judge's activism score, the presence of discretionary docket control, the presence of the state government as a party to the case, the judge's ideology, and experience in a non–judicial elected office is presented in Table 5.3. The model's diagnostic statistics are strong. The logistic regression model correctly predicted the dependent variable 79% of the time. The probability of obtaining a Wald Chi Square test statistic of 14.9 is 0.0%, which leads to the conclusion that at least one of the regression coefficients in the model is not equal to zero. In

**Table 5.3** Logistic regression of judges' Vote to Strike Law as Unconstitutional

| Variable | Coefficient (Std. error) | Marginal effect (%) |
|---|---|---|
| **Independent variables** | | |
| Judge's 'Activism' score | 0.086* (0.053) | +14.5 |
| Court's discretionary docket control | 1.184*** (0.348) | +30.4 |
| State government party to case | −1.095** (0.495) | −18.3 |
| Judge's ideological score | 0.265 (0.311) | |
| Elected, non–judicial experience | −0.236 (0.292) | |
| Constant | −1.834*** (0.560) | |
| **Model diagnostics** | | |
| Number of observations[a] | 262 | |
| Wald $chi^2_{(df=5)}$ | 14.940 | |
| Probability > $chi^2$ | 0.011 | |
| McKelvey & Zavoina's $R^2$ | 0.269 | |

*Note* Numbers in parentheses are robust standard errors clustered on case citation. Case citation was chosen to cluster on because it best allows for differences in individual cases. Alternative models with robust standard errors clustered on state and judge are provided in Tables 5.6 and 5.7 in the Appendix. Marginal effects are calculated by altering the statistically significant variables from their minimum to their maximum. $*p< 0.1$, $**p< 0.05$, $***p< 0.01$

[a] An ideological score is not available for one judge in the dataset, therefore this judge's votes are excluded from the analysis

addition, the model's McKelvey and Zavoina's $R^2$ is 26.9% and the proportional reduction in error is 9.8%.[31]

Three of the five variables are statistically significant and in the expected direction. Most important to this research, of course, is the effect that a judge's 'activism' score has on his or her vote in judicial review cases. As hypothesized, the model indicates that the higher a judge's 'activism' score is, the more likely he or she is to strike down a state or local law as unconstitutional. In fact, the effect of this variable is that the most 'activist' judge (one with an 'activism' score of +2) is 14.5% more likely to strike a state or local law as unconstitutional than is the least 'activist' judge (one with an 'activism' score of −9). Figure 5.1 plots the marginal effect of a judge's 'activism' score on his or her vote to strike a state or local law as unconstitutional.

Also significant and in the expected direction are two of the four control variables. First included was the court–specific variable that indicated whether the court has a

[31] See Chap. 4 for a discussion of the McKelvey and Zavoina's $R^2$.

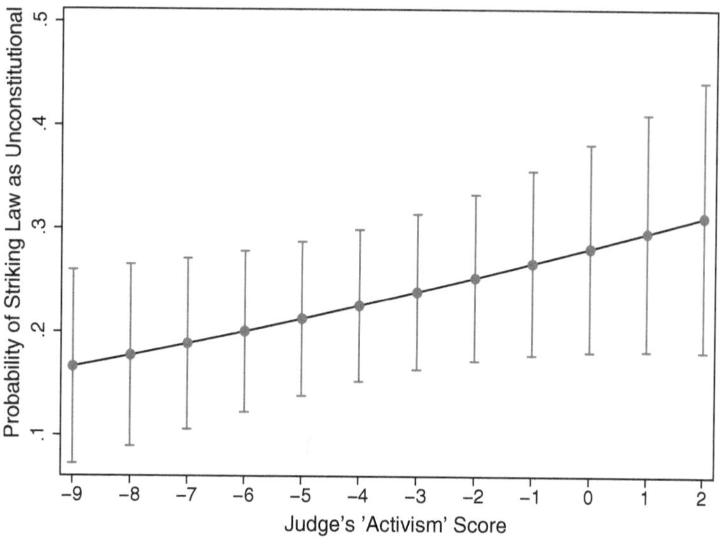


**Fig. 5.1** Predictive margins (with 95% confidence intervals) for *activismScore* variable

discretionary docket. The presence of a discretionary docket increases the likelihood of a vote to strike a state or local law as unconstitutional. The effect of this variable is that a judge who serves in a court with a discretionary docket is 30.4% more likely to strike a state or local law as unconstitutional than is a judge who serves in a court without a discretionary docket. Figure 5.2 plots the marginal effect of the presence of a discretionary docket on the likelihood of a judge voting to strike a state or local law as unconstitutional. These findings are quite consistent with Eisenberg and Miller's (2009) findings that state high courts reverse 28.1% of cases under mandatory jurisdiction and 51.6% of cases under discretionary jurisdiction.

The second control variable included was the case–specific variable that indicated whether the state government was a party to the suit. The state government being a party to a case decreases the likelihood of a vote to strike a state or local law as unconstitutional. The effect of this variable is that a judge who is hearing a case where the state government is a party is 18.3% less likely to strike a state or local law as unconstitutional than is a judge who is hearing a case where the state government is not a party. Figure 5.3 plots the marginal effect of the presence of the state government as a party to the case on the likelihood of a judge voting to strike a state or local law as unconstitutional. These findings are consistent with the litigant resources arguments of Scigliano (1971), Galanter (1974), Segal (1988), Emmert (1992), McGuire (1995), and Collins (2004).

Not statistically significant are the two judge–level variables controlling for the judge's ideology and exploring the effect that non–judicial elected experience have on judge's votes in judicial review cases. The former result, consistent with Howard's (1977) findings for federal appellate judges, gives us the confidence to say that the

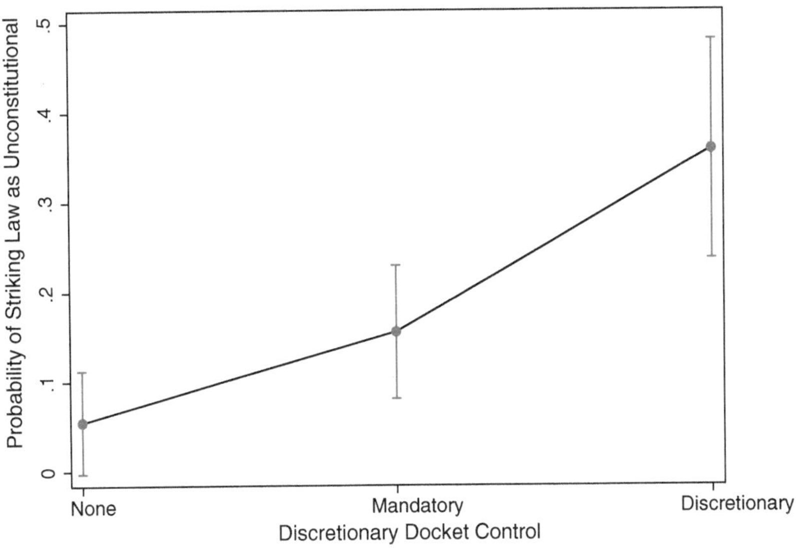


**Fig. 5.2** Predictive margins (with 95% confidence intervals) for *discertionary* variable

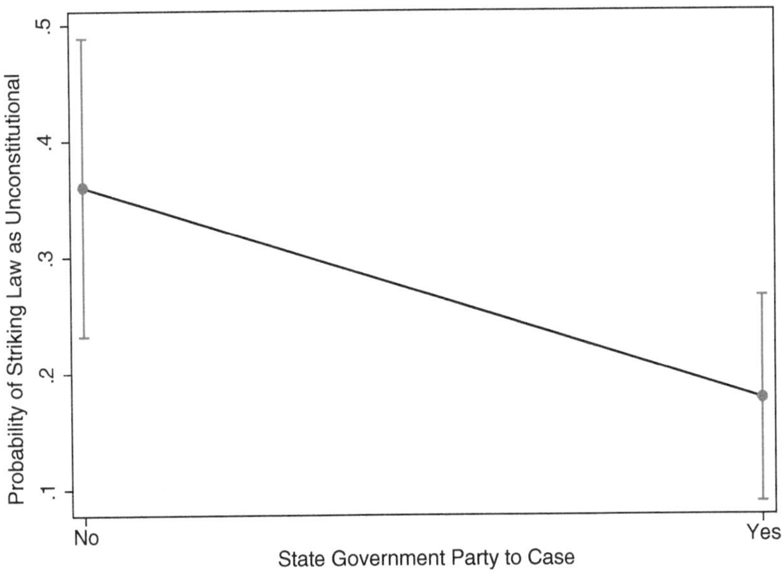


**Fig. 5.3** Predictive margins (with 95% confidence intervals) for *stateGov* variable

statistically significant relationship between the judge's vote on the constitutionality of state and local laws and the judge's 'activism' is not merely a proxy of the judge's ideology. Rather the judge's 'activism' score is a significant predictor of the judge's vote, even when a model of judicial review decisions controls for the judge's ideology.

For the latter judge–level variable, while there are theoretical reasons to expect that political experience might effect judges' behavior,[32] no such effect was found in this model. There could be several reasons for this finding. First, the type of behavior affected by non–judicial elected experience might not be a judge's decision in judicial review cases. Maybe, instead, the behavior that this type of experience affects is decision–making in another type of case. Or, perhaps instead, the affected type of behavior is the choice of which cases to accept for review. Second, it could be that operationalizing political experience as non–judicial elected office is too limiting. Perhaps service in politically appointed non–judicial positions and activity with political parties and organizaitons should be included in the operationalization as well.

## 5.4 Conclusion

Clearly, many factors affect a state high court judge's vote in judicial review cases. Emmert (1992) creates an integrated model that includes issue area, litigant resources, legal arguments raised, and lower court ruling for explaining these cases. Langer (2002, 2003) supposes an ideological zone within which state high court judges are free to strike down laws as unconstitutional. Once a judge leaves that ideological zone, however, judges might face retribution from other actors. A variable that has not before been considered by scholars of judicial review in the states is one that captures the judges' role orientations.[33]

This chapter began by arguing that the judicial role orientation matters only to the extent to which it affects judicial behavior. The results from a model that builds on the existing literature and takes into account judges' role orientations are quite promising. When the judicial role orientation is operationalized on the 'activism–restraintist' spectrum, it is clear that the judges' role orientations exert a statistically significant effect on their decision on the constitutionality of legislation, so much so that the most 'activist' judge is 14.5% more likely to strike down a law as unconstitutional than is the most 'restraintist' judge. Moreover, and as expected, the degree to which judges can control their docket increases the likelihood that the judges will vote to strike down laws as unconstitutional. Conversely, when the state government is a party to a case, judges are much less likely to strike down laws as unconstitutional. Consistent with Langer's (2002) expectation, no judge who was subjected to reappointment by

[32] See, for example, Baum (1997), Gryski and Main (1986), and (Nagel, 1961).

[33] This is not to say that these previously considered variables are not relevant in a judge's decision in judicial review cases. Rather, as has been argued here, a judge's view about the propriety of striking down laws as unconstitutional should also be considered.

the governor or legislature votes to strike down a law as unconstitutional during the period in question. Finally, combined, these variables correctly predict a judge's vote to declare a law unconstitutional 79% of the time.

## Appendix

The analysis conducted in this chapter required the collection of variables relating to the judicial decision–making of survey respondents. The universe of relevant cases was identified by conducting a LexisNexis search for cases decided in 2011 in which the term "!constitution!" appears in either LexisNexis' Procedural Posture, Overview, or Outcome section and either the term "affirmed" or "reversed" appears in LexisNexis' Outcome section.[34] Using the term "!constitution!" instructed LexisNexis to return all those cases that, in the designated sections, contain the word "constitutional," regardless of prefix or suffix.[35] Using "affirmed" or "reversed" limited the cases returned to those in which the merits of the case was resolved in a definitive fashion. Provided in this Appendix is: (1) a list of cases included in this chapter's analysis, including the state or local laws challenged as unconstitutional (Table 5.4); (2) the codebook for this data collection; and (3) alternatively specified models using the presence of an intermediate appellate court as a proxy for discretionary docket control (Table 5.5), this chapter's model clustered on state (Table 5.6), and this chapter's model clustered on judge (Table 5.7).

## Codebook

### *Identification Variables*

**judgeID**[36]
A four digit variable to uniquely identify each judge in the dataset. The first two numbers identify the state. The third and fourth numbers correspond with the judge's randomly assigned identification number.

[34]The exact search phrase was: "DATE AFT(12/31/2010) AND DATE BEF(01/01/2012) AND POSTURE(constitution!) OR POSTURE(unconstitution!) OR OVERVIEW(constitution!) OR OVERVIEW(unconstitution!) OR OUTCOME(constitution!) OR OUTCOME(unconstitution!) AND OUTCOME(affirmed) OR OUTCOME(reversed)."

[35]This returns, for example, "constitutional," "constitutionality," "unconstitutional," etc.

[36]As per the survey's promise of confidentiality, identification variables will need to be removed from the dataset before shared or otherwise made publicly available.

**judgeName**[37]
A string variable to identify the last name and first initial of each judge in the dataset.

**citation**
A string variable to identify each case in the dataset by regional reporter citation.

**petitioner**
A string variable to identify the petitioner in the case.

**respondent**
A string variable to identify the respondent in the case.

**decisionDate**
A variable to identify the date the court announced its decision in the case.

## *Background Variables*

**issueArea**
A variable to identify the subject matter of the constitutional controversy.

```
Miscellaneous = 4
Economic activity and economic regulation = 3
Criminal law and criminal procedure = 2
Civil liberty and civil right = 1
```

**stateGov**
A dichotomous variable to indicate whether the state government is a party to the case.

```
yes = 1
no = 0
```

**stateGovPetitioner**
A dichotomous variable to indicate whether the state is seeking state supreme court review.

```
yes = 1
no = 0
```

[37] As per the survey's promise of confidentiality, identification variables will need to be removed from the dataset before shared or otherwise made publicly available.

**stateGovRespondent**
A dichotomous variable to indicate whether the state is opposing state supreme court review.

```
yes = 1
no = 0
```

## *Outcome Variables*

**majVotes**
A variable to indicate the number of judges voting in the majority.

**minVotes**
A variable to indicate the number of judges voting in dissent.

**minWinningCoalition**
A variable to indicate whether the case was won by one vote.

```
yes = 1
no = 0
```

**decisionDirection**
A variable to indicate the ideological direction of the court's decision.[38]

```
liberal = 2
conservative = 1
```

**declarationUncon**
A dichotomous variable to indicate whether the court declared a state law or a local ordinance unconstitutional.

```
yes = 1
no = 0
```

**disposition**
A dichotomous variable to indicate whether the court affirmed the decision of the trial court.

```
yes = 1
no = 0
```

---

[38]Consistent with Spaeth et al. (2013), for all ideologically–orientated variables, a liberal outcome in the context of issues relating to civil liberties and civil rights or criminal law and criminal procedure is defined as:

**vote**

A variable to indicate the judge's level of agreement with the outcome of the case.

```
dissented = 3
filed a concurrence = 2
voted with majority/plurality = 1
```

**direction**[5]

A variable to indicate the ideological direction of the judge's vote.

```
liberal = 2
conservative = 1
```

---

(Footnote 38 continued)

- anti–government in the context of due process, except where otherwise noted
- pro–accountability and/or anti–corruption in campaign spending
- pro–affirmative action
- pro–child or juvenile
- pro–civil liberties or civil rights claimant
- pro–female in abortion
- pro–government, anti–owner in takings
- pro–Indian
- pro–indigent
- pro–person accused or convicted of crime, or denied a jury trial
- pro–privacy
- pro–underdog

In the context of issues relating to economic activity and economic regulation:
- anti–business
- anti–employer
- anti–union member or employee vis–a–vis union
- anti–union in union antitrust
- anti–union in union or closed shop
- pro–accountability in governmental corruption

(Footnote 38 continued)
- pro–bankrupt
- pro–competition
- pro–consumer
- pro–debtor
- pro–economic underdog
- pro–environmental protection
- pro–government
- pro–indigent
- pro–injured person
- pro–small business vis–a–vis large business
- pro–state in state tax cases
- pro–trial in arbitration
- pro–union, except where otherwise noted.

**Table 5.4** State and local laws challenged as unconstitutional in 2011

| State | Case citation | Challenged law |
|---|---|---|
| Alabama | 68 So.3d 99 | 2009 Ala. Acts 768 |
| Alabama | 69 So.3d 827 | 2009 Ala. Acts 811 |
| Alabama | 73 So.3d 634 | Ala. Code §30-3-4.1 |
| Alaska | 251 P.3d 341 | Alaska Stat. §12.55.120 |
| Arkansas | 380 S.W.3d 429 | Ark. Code Ann. §§9-8-301 to -305 |
| Arkansas | 384 S.W.3d 488 | Ark. Code Ann. §§5-4-105 and 16-93-301 to -303 |
| Arkansas | 384 S.W.3d 534 | Ark. Code Ann. §16-42-101 |
| Arkansas | 385 S.W.3d 810 | Ark. Code Ann. §24-11-102 |
| Arkansas | 385 S.W.3d 822 | Ark. Code Ann. §16-55-208 |
| California | 247 P.3d 112 | Cal. Water Code §1525 |
| California | 257 P.3d 72 | Ca. Penal Code §140 |
| Connecticut | 22 A.3d 1262 | Conn. Gen. Stat. §53a-193 |
| Connecticut | 24 A.3d 1243 | Conn. Gen. Stat. §53-21 |
| Delaware | 15 A.3d 1247 | Del. Code Ann. tit. 10, §8145 |
| Delaware | 28 A.3d 1037 | Del. Code Ann. tit. 6, §18-1002 |
| Florida | 73 So.3d 120 | Fla. Stat. §774.206 |
| Florida | 73 So.3d 151 | Fla. Stat. §29.008 |
| Georgia | 710 S.E.2d 773 | Ga. Code Ann. §20-2-2081 |
| Georgia | 711 S.E.2d 665 | Ga. Code Ann. §17-7-131 |
| Georgia | 711 S.E.2d 709 | Ga. Code Ann. §46-3-204 |
| Georgia | 712 S.E.2d 820 | Ga. Code Ann. §9-13-172 |
| Georgia | 712 S.E.2d 838 | Ga. Code Ann. §16-10-20 |
| Georgia | 713 S.E.2d 846 | Ga. Code Ann. §48-8-100 |
| Idaho | 264 P.3d 907 | Lewiston, Idaho, Ordinance No. 4512 |
| Idaho | 265 P.3d 495 | Idaho Code Ann. §32-717 |
| Illinois | 942 N.E.2d 1235 | 725 Ill. Comp. Stat. 5/115-10 |
| Illinois | 948 N.E.2d 70 | 735 Ill. Comp. Stat. 5/22-105 |
| Illinois | 953 N.E.2d 899 | 2009 Ill. Laws 34-38 |
| Illinois | 957 N.E.2d 876 | 625 Ill. Comp. Stat. 35/6 |
| Illinois | 960 N.E.2d 1071 | 720 Comp. Stat. 5/36-1 to -4 |
| Indiana | 959 N.E.2d 794 | Ind. Code §§24-5-14-1 to -13 |
| Kansas | 247 P.3d 1043 | Kan. Stat. Ann. §21-4721 |
| Kansas | 249 P.3d 444 | Kan. Stat. Ann. §§74-8702, -8750, and -8761 |
| Kansas | 256 P.3d 845 | Kan. Stat. Ann. §8-1012 |
| Kansas | 264 P.3d 102 | Kan. Stat. Ann. §40-2910 |
| Kentucky | 345 S.W.3d 811 | Campbell Co., Ordinances 8-04 and 20-04 |
| Kentucky | 364 S.W.3d 455 | Ky. Rev. Stat. Ann. §342.316 |
| Maine | 26 A.3d 850 | Me. Rev. Stat. tit. 17-A, §2(8) |

(continued)

**Table 5.4** (continued)

| State | Case citation | Challenged law |
|---|---|---|
| Maryland | 10 A.3d 1167 | Md. Code Ann., Pub. Safety §5-301 |
| Maryland | 30 A.3d 962 | Md. Code Ann., Real Prop. §8-701 |
| Massachusetts | 953 N.E.2d 691 | Mass. Gen. Laws ch. 110A, §301 |
| Massachusetts | 958 N.E.2d 25 | Mass. Gen. Laws ch. 269, 10 |
| Michigan | 803 N.W.2d 674 | Mich. Comp. Laws §211.34 |
| Minnesota | 798 N.W.2d 517 | Minn. Stat. §609.535 |
| Mississippi | 55 So.3d 1068 | Miss. Code Ann. §75-24-25 |
| Mississippi | 70 So.3d 204 | Miss. Code Ann. §27-77-7 |
| Missouri | 332 S.W.3d 115 | Mo. Rev. Stat. §632.495 |
| Missouri | 343 S.W.3d 656 | Mo. Rev. Stat. §99.1205 |
| Missouri | 344 S.W.3d 160 | Mo. Rev. Stat. §339.010 |
| Missouri | 344 S.W.3d 193 | Mo. Rev. Stat. §566.151 |
| Montana | 248 P.3d 813 | Mont. Code Ann. §61-8-402 |
| Montana | 248 P.3d 826 | Mont. Code Ann. §46-18-202 |
| Montana | 249 P.3d 913 | Mont. Code Ann. §39-71-411 and -724 |
| Montana | 260 P.3d 133 | Mont. Code Ann. §76-2-205 |
| Montana | 261 P.3d 1009 | Mont. Code Ann. §45-7-306 |
| Montana | 271 P.3d 1 | Mont. Code Ann. §13-35-227 |
| Nevada | 251 P.3d 163 | Nev. Rev. Stat. §3.223 |
| Nevada | 255 P.3d 247 | Nev. Assemb. B. 6, §18 |
| Nevada | 255 P.3d 262 | Nev. Rev. Stat. §484C.340 |
| Nevada | 261 P.3d 1067 | Nev. Rev. Stat. 200.710 |
| New Hampshire | 13 A.3d 145 | N.H. Rev. Stat. Ann. §9:16 |
| New Hampshire | 20 A.3d 961 | N.H. Rev. Stat. Ann. §100-A:54 |
| New York | 953 N.E.2d 753 | N.Y. Elec. Law §16-102 |
| North Dakota | 803 N.W.2d 587 | N.D. Cent. Code §50-25.1 |
| North Dakota | 803 N.W.2d 601 | N.D. Cent. Code §65-05-09 |
| Ohio | 950 N.E.2d 528 | Ohio Rev. Code Ann. §2907.02 |
| Ohio | 951 N.E.2d 766 | Ohio Rev. Code Ann. §2901.08 |
| Ohio | 952 N.E.2d 1108 | Ohio Rev. Code Ann. §2907.04 |
| Ohio | 958 N.E.2d 169 | Ohio Rev. Code Ann. §4117.02 |
| Oklahoma | 260 P.3d 1251 | Okla. Stat. tit. 22, §171.2 |
| Pennsylvania | 30 A.3d 1083 | Bedminster Township, Pa., Ordinance 118 |
| Pennsylvania | 30 A.3d 381 | 42 Pa. Cons. Stat. §9711 |
| Pennsylvania | 31 A.3d 668 | 42 Pa. Cons. Stat. §9711 |
| Rhode Island | 15 A.3d 565 | R.I. Gen. Laws §45-9-1 |
| South Carolina | 705 S.E.2d 53 | S.C. Code Ann. §63-19-2440 |
| South Carolina | 706 S.E.2d 16 | S.C. Code Ann. §14-7-1820 |
| South Carolina | 712 S.E.2d 401 | S.C. Code Ann. §15-78-120 |

(continued)

**Table 5.4** (continued)

| State | Case citation | Challenged law |
|---|---|---|
| South Carolina | 712 S.E.2d 416 | S.C. Code Ann. §5-1-30 |
| South Carolina | 719 S.E.2d 660 | Columbia, S.C., City Code §17-55 |
| South Dakota | 797 N.W.2d 47 | S.D. Codified Laws §41-6-33 |
| South Dakota | 802 N.W.2d 165 | S.D. Codified Laws §§22-24B-22 and -24 |
| South Dakota | 802 N.W.2d 905 | Sioux Falls, S.D., Municipal Code §2-60 |
| South Dakota | 804 N.W.2d 618 | S.D. Codified Laws §13-13-10 |
| Tennessee | 333 S.W.3d 59 | Tenn. Code Ann. §67-4-2004 |
| Texas | 340 S.W.3d 717 | Tex. Code Crim. Proc. Ann. art. 37.071 |
| Texas | 347 S.W.3d 277 | Tex. Bus. & Com. Code Ann. §102.052 |
| Texas | 351 S.W.3d 315 | Tex. Code Crim. Proc. Ann. art. 38.071 |
| Utah | 245 P.3d 745 | Utah Code Ann. §78A-6-701 |
| Vermont | 26 A.3d 37 | Vt. Rules Civil Proc. 80.6 |
| Virginia | 704 S.E.2d 365 | 8 Va. Admin. Code §35-60-20 |
| Virginia | 719 S.E.2d 294 | Va. Code Ann. 33.1-221.1 |
| Washington | 246 P.3d 1224 | Wash. Enforcement Law. Cons. Rules 10.14 |
| Washington | 246 P.3d 1254 | Wash. Rev. Code §34.05.449 |
| Washington | 251 P.3d 877 | Wash. Rev. Code §9A.76.020 |
| Washington | 257 P.3d 648 | Wash. Rev. Code §2.36.050 |
| Washington | 267 P.3d 305 | Snohomish Co., Wash., Code §10.01.040 |
| West Virginia | 2011 W. Va. LEXIS 526 | W. Va. Code §62-12-26 |
| West Virginia | 2011 W. Va. LEXIS 561 | W. Va. Code §62-12-26 |
| West Virginia | 2011 W. Va. LEXIS 682 | W. Va. Code §5-16D-6 |
| West Virginia | 710 S.E.2d 98 | W. Va. Code §62-12-26 |
| West Virginia | 715 S.E.2d 405 | W. Va. Code §55-7B-8 |
| West Virginia | 725 S.E.2d 756 | W. Va. Code R. §§191-2-1, -4.11, and -3-3 |
| Wyoming | 246 P.3d 864 | Wyo. Stat. Ann. §§31-7-305 and -307 |
| Wyoming | 256 P.3d 536 | Wyo. Stat. Ann. §6-2-501 |
| Wyoming | 258 P.3d 720 | Wyo. Stat. Ann. §12-8-301 |
| Wyoming | 262 P.3d 1263 | Wyo. Stat. Ann. §27-14-108 |

*Source* LexisNexis

**Table 5.5** Logistic regression of Judges' vote to strike law as unconstitutional using intermediate appellate Court

| Variable | Coefficient (std. error) | Marginal effect (%) |
|---|---|---|
| **Independent variables** | | |
| Judge's 'Activism' Score | 0.091* (0.054) | +16.0 |
| State has intermediate appellate court | 1.883*** (0.669) | +23.4 |
| State government party to case | −1.025** (0.493) | −18.0 |
| Judge's Ideological Score | 0.029 (0.345) | |
| Elected, non–judicial experience | −0.205 (0.284) | |
| Constant | −1.685** (0.701) | |
| **Model diagnostics** | | |
| Number of observations | 262 | |
| Wald chi$^2$ $(df=5)$ | 19.140 | |
| Probability > chi$^2$ | 0.001 | |
| McKelvey & Zavoina's $R^2$ | 0.221 | |

*Note* Numbers in parentheses are robust standard errors clustered on case citation. Marginal effects are calculated by altering the statistically significant variables from their minimum to their maximum. $^*p<0.1$, $^{**}p<0.05$, $^{***}p<0.01$

**Table 5.6** Logistic regression of judges' vote to strike law as unconstitutional clustered by state

| Variable | Coefficient (std. error) | Marginal effect (%) |
|---|---|---|
| **Independent variables** | | |
| Judge's 'Activism' score | 0.086 (0.068) | |
| Court's discretionary docket control | 1.184*** (0.330) | +30.4 |
| State government party to case | −1.095** (0.489) | −18.3 |
| Judge's ideological score | 0.265 (0.318) | |
| Elected, non–judicial experience | −0.236 (0.433) | |
| Constant | −1.834*** (0.589) | |
| **Model diagnostics** | | |
| Number of observations | 262 | |
| Wald chi$^2$ $(df=5)$ | 19.990 | |
| Probability > chi$^2$ | 0.001 | |
| McKelvey & Zavoina's $R^2$ | 0.269 | |

*Note* Numbers in parentheses are robust standard errors clustered on state. Marginal effects are calculated by altering the statistically significant variables from their minimum to their maximum. $^*p<0.1$, $^{**}p<0.05$, $^{***}p<0.01$

**Table 5.7** Logistic regression of Judges' vote to strike law as unconstitutional clustered by Judge

| Variable | Coefficient (std. error) | Marginal effect (%) |
|---|---|---|
| **Independent variables** | | |
| Judge's 'Activism' Score | 0.086<br>(0.085) | |
| Court's discretionary docket control | 1.184***<br>(0.239) | +30.4 |
| State government party to case | −1.095***<br>(0.323) | −18.3 |
| Judge's Ideological Score | 0.265<br>(0.243) | |
| Elected, non–judicial experience | −0.236<br>(0.392) | |
| Constant | −1.834***<br>(0.607) | |
| **Model diagnostics** | | |
| Number of Observations | 262 | |
| Wald chi$^2$ $_{(df=5)}$ | 54.180 | |
| Probability > chi$^2$ | 0.000 | |
| McKelvey & Zavoina's $R^2$ | 0.269 | |

*Note* Numbers in parentheses are robust standard errors clustered on judge. Marginal effects are calculated by altering the statistically significant variables from their minimum to their maximum. *$p<0.1$, **$p<0.05$, ***$p<0.01$

# References


Baum, Lawrence. 1994. "What Judges Want: Judges' Goals and Judicial Behavior." *Political Research Quarterly* 47(3): 749–768.

Baum, Lawrence. 1997. *The Puzzle of Judicial Behavior*. Ann Arbor: University of Michigan Press.

Becker, Theodore L. 1966. "A Survey Study of Hawaiian Judges: The Effect on Decisions of Judicial Role Variations." *American Political Science Review* 60(3): 677–680.

Biddle, Bruce J. 1979. *Role Theory: Expectations, Identities, and Behaviors*. New York: Academic.

Biddle, Bruce J. 1986. "Recent Developments in Role Theory." *Annual Review of Sociology* 12: 67–92.

Bonica, Adam, and Michael J. Woodruff. 2012. "State Supreme Court Ideology and "New Style" Judicial Campaigns." Stanford University. Typescript.

Bureau of Justice Statistics. 2000. "State Court Organization." http://www.bjs.gov/content/pub/pdf/sco9804.pdf (November 4, 2014).

Collins, Jr., Paul M. 2004. "Friends of the Court: Examining the Influence of Amicus Curiae Participation in U.S. Supreme Court Litigation." *Law & Society Review* 38(4): 807–832.

Eisenberg, Theodore, and Geoffrey P. Miller. 2009. "Reversal, Dissent, and Variability in State Supreme Courts: The Centrality of Jurisdictional Source." *Boston University Law Review* 89: 1451–1504.

Emmert, Craig F. 1992. "An Integrated Case-Related Model of Judicial Decision Making: Explaining State Supreme Court Decisions in Judicial Review Cases." *Journal of Politics* 54(2): 543–552.

Emmert, Craig F., and Carol Ann Traut. 1992. "State Supreme Courts, State Constitutions, and Judicial Policymaking." *Justice System Journal* 16(1): 37–48.

Galanter, Marc. 1974. "Why the 'Haves' Come Out Ahead: Speculations on the Limits of Legal Change." *Law & Society Review* 9(1): 95–160.

Gibson, James L. 1977. "Discriminant Functions, Role Orientations and Judicial Behavior: Theoretical and Methodological Linkages." *Journal of Politics* 39(4): 984–1007.
Gibson, James L. 1978. "Judges' Role Orientations, Attitudes, and Decisions: An Interactive Model." *American Political Science Review* 72(3): 911–924.
Gibson, James L. 1981b. "The Role Concept in Judicial Research." *Law & Policy* 3(3): 291–311.
Glick, Henry R., and Craig F. Emmert. 1986. "Stability and Change: Characteristics of State Supreme Court Judges." *Judicature* 70(2): 107–112.
Gryski, Gerard S., and Eleanor C. Main. 1986. "Social Backgrounds as Predictors of Votes on State Courts of Last Resort: The Case of Sex Discrimination." *Western Political Quarterly* 39(3): 528–537.
Howard, Jr., J. Woodford. 1977. "Role Perceptions and Behavior in Three U.S. Courts of Appeals." *Journal of Politics* 39(4): 916–938.
James, Dorothy B. 1968. "Role Theory and the Supreme Court." *Journal of Politics* 30(1): 160–186.
Jaros, Dean, and Robert I. Mendelsohn. 1967. "The Judicial Role and Sentencing Behavior." *Midwest Journal of Political Science* 11(4): 471–488.
Jewell, Malcolm E. 1970. "Attitudinal Determinants of Legislative Behavior: The Utility of Role Analysis." In *Legislatures in Developmental Perspective*, ed. Allan Kornberg, and Lloyd D. Musolf. Durham: Duke University Press pp. 460–500.
Langer, Laura. 2002. *Judicial Review in State Supreme Courts: A Comparative Study*. Albany: State University of New York Press.
Langer, Laura. 2003. "Strategic Considerations and Judicial Review: The Case of Workers' Compensation Laws in the American States." *Public Choice* 116(1/2): 55–78.
McGuire, Kevin T. 1995. "Repeat Players in the Supreme Court: The Role of Experienced Lawyers in Litigation Success." *Journal of Politics* 57(1): 187–196.
Murphy, Walter. 1964. *Elements of Judicial Strategy*. Chicago: University of Chicago Press.
Nagel, Stuart S. 1961. "Political Party Affiliation and Judges' Decisions." *American Political Science Review* 55(4): 843–850.
Porter, Mary Cornelia. 1982. "State Supreme Courts and the Legacy of the Warren Court: Some Inquiries for a New Situation." In *State Supreme Courts: Policymakers in the Federal System*, ed. Mary Cornelia Porter, and G. Alan Tarr. Westport: Greenwood.
Posner, Richard A. 2006. "The Role of the Judge in the Twenty-First Century." *Boston University Law Review* 86(5): 1049–1068.
Rohde, David W., and Harold J. Spaeth. 1976. *Supreme Court Decision Making*. San Francisco: W. H. Freeman and Company.
Scheb, II, John M., Terry Bowen, and Gary Anderson. 1991. "Ideology, Role Orientations, and Behavior in the State Courts of Last Resort." *American Politics Quarterly* 19(3): 324–335.
Scigliano, Robert. 1971. *The Supreme Court and the Presidency*. New York: Free Press.
Segal, Jeffrey A. 1984. "Predicting Supreme Court Cases Probabilistically: The Search and Seizure Cases, 1962–1981." *American Political Science Review* 78(4): 891–900.
Segal, Jeffrey A. 1988. "Amicus Curiae Briefs by the Solicitor General During the Warren and Burger Courts." *Western Political Quarterly* 41(1): 135–144.
Spaeth, Harold J., Sara Benesh, Lee Epstein, Andrew D. Martin, Jeffrey A. Segal, and Theodore J. Ruger. 2013. "Supreme Court Database, Version 2013 Release 01." http://supremecourtdatabase.org (December 1, 2012).
Tanenhaus, Joseph, Marvin Schick, Matthew Muraskin, and Daniel Rosen. 1963. "The Supreme Court's Certiorari Jurisdiction: Cue Theory." In *Judicial Decision-Making*, ed. Glendon Schubert. New York: Free Press.
Tarr, G. Alan, and Mary C. Porter. 1988. *State Supreme Courts in State and Nation*. New Haven: Yale University Press.
Teger, Stuart H., and Douglas Kosinski. 1980. "The Cue Theory of Supreme Court Certiorari Jurisdiction: A Reconsideration." *Journal of Politics* 42(3): 834–846.
Thomas, Edwin J., and Bruce J. Biddle. 1966. "The Nature and History of Role Theory." In *Role Theory: Concepts and Research*, ed. Bruce J. Biddle, and Edwin J. Thomas. New York: John Wiley & Sons.

# Chapter 6
# Concluding Thoughts

On September 5, 2005, President George W. Bush nominated then–U.S. Court of Appeals Judge John Roberts to serve as Chief Justice of the United States. One week later, the Judiciary Committee of the United States Senate began its confirmation hearings on Roberts' nomination (Greenhouse 2005). Roberts' prepared remarks for the Committee turned almost immediately to his belief about the function judges serve in society. He began, "My personal appreciation that I owe a great debt to others reinforces my view that a certain humility should characterize the judicial role" (U.S. Congress. Senate. Committee on the Judiciary 2005). Roberts continued, "Judges and Justices are servants of the law, not the other way around. Judges are like umpires. Umpires dont make the rules, they apply them. The role of an umpire and a judge is critical. They make sure everybody plays by the rules, but it is a limited role. Nobody ever went to a ball game to see the umpire (U.S. Congress. Senate. Committee on the Judiciary 2005)."

Many of the senators seemed quite pleased with Roberts' characterization of the judicial role (Purdum and Toner 2005). During his statement on Roberts' nomination, Senator Jefferson Sessions expressed his satisfaction by proclaiming, "What we must have, what our legal system demands, is a fair and unbiased umpire, one who calls the game according to the existing rules and does so competently and honestly every day. This is the American ideal of law" (U.S. Congress. Senate. Committee on the Judiciary 2005). Likewise, Senator Samuel Brownback said,

> In today's American governance, the legislature can pass a bill, and the Executive can sign it, but then everybody holds their breath, waiting to see how the Court is going to look at this and how it is going to interpret it. It seems as if the Court is the real mover of what the actual law is. And that is a bad thing. The umpire should call the ball fair or foul, it is in or it is out, but not become actively involved as a player on the field. Unfortunately, we have reached a point where, in many respects, the judiciary is the most active policy player on the field (U.S. Congress. Senate. Committee on the Judiciary 2005).


R.V. Carman, Jr., *Making Good Law or Good Policy?*,
DOI 10.1007/978-3-319-53381-0_6

The judge–umpire trope was so popular during the hearings that followed the prepared remarks and statements, that the word "umpire" appears 28 times in the official hearing transcript (U.S. Congress. Senate. Committee on the Judiciary 2005).

Roberts' was not the first use of the judge–umpire analogy. Kerr (2008) explains that it can be traced back to baseball's earliest days.[1] Indeed, in finding that a trial court judge could prevent a witness from answering a leading question even though the prosecution had not objected, the Louisiana Supreme Court wrote that a "trial is not a mere lutte between counsel, in which the judge sits merely as an umpire to decide disputes which may arise between them" (State v. Crittenden 1886).[2]

The first documented case of a U.S. Supreme Court justice using the analogy occurred in 1951. In an address on why Learned and Augustus Hand were great judges, Justice Robert Jackson explained "the test of an independent judiciary is a simple one—the one you would apply in choosing an umpire for a baseball game. What do you ask of him? You do not ask that he shall never make a mistake or always agree with you, or always support the home team. You want an umpire who calls them as he sees them" (Jackson 1951).

So, while Roberts did not coin the judge–umpire analogy, his use of it has brought the debate over the proper function of judges into the public consciousness. In some circles it has also become the de facto standard by which some seek to hold all those being considered for judicial office. For example, during the next series of U.S. Supreme Court confirmation hearings, supporters of then–U.S. Court of Appeals Judge Samuel Alito explained, "When you take that judicial oath, you become a different person. You decide cases not to reach the result that you would like, but based on what the facts and the law command" (U.S. Congress. Senate. Committee on the Judiciary 2006).

However, others have questioned the simplicity of the judge–umpire analogy. For example, U.S. Court of Appeals Judge Theodore McKee (2006, 1710–1715) wrote, "[W]e have now been saddled with an image of judges who are able to ignore the many kinds of bias that affect everyone else and discharge their duties in a mechanical manner that is removed from the society and its many forces... In the final analysis, judicial objectivity can not be achieved unless we judges recognize that we have been exposed to the same social afflictions as everyone else, and that our immunity may be no stronger than anyone else's."

Likewise, asked to comment on the judge–umpire analogy during her own U.S. Supreme Court confirmation hearings, then–U.S. Solicitor General Elena Kagan explained, "like all metaphors, it does have its limits" (U.S. Congress. Senate. Committee on the Judiciary 2010). Kagan went on to voice concern that the judge–umpire analogy might suggest that law is "a kind of robotic enterprise, that there's a kind of automatic quality to it, that it's easy, that we just sort of stand there and, you know,

---

[1]For an excellent discussion of the judge–umpire analogy, see Zelinsky (2010).

[2]Zelinsky (2010, 115) explains that, as baseball was a relatively young sport at that time and professional baseball umpires had only been introduced seven years earlier, the court referenced the more familiar wrestling umpire and "referred to the sport by its French name, lutte."

we go ball and strike, and everything is clear–cut and that there is no judgment in the process" (U.S. Congress. Senate. Committee on the Judiciary 2010).

While this analogy and these exchanges do not use the technical language of role theory and its concept of role orientation, introduced in Chap. 2, they are, at their very core, a normative discussion of just that—the proper professional behavior for judges. These anecdotes serve to provide us a reminder of the pervasiveness, if sometimes obscurity, of discourse around the appropriate judicial role orientation. What follows in this final chapter is a recounting of this work's main findings, a summary of the implications of these findings, and a discussion of the potential for future research.

## 6.1 Summary of the Findings

This work contributes to our understanding of state high court judges in several important ways. First, it explains, theoretically, how role orientations *should* affect these judges. In Chap. 2, a conceptualization and operationalization of the judicial role orientation was built, grounded in the role theoretic literature. Role theory argues that institutional structure, coupled with the expectations of relevant others and one's own expectations synthesize together into a role orientation. This led to the conceptualization of the judicial role orientation as the stimuli that a judge feels can legitimately be allowed to influence his or her decision–making and, in the case of conflict among influences, what priorities to assign to different decisional criteria. Following logically from this conceptualization, and grounded in the judicial 'activism' literature, this study operationalized judges' role orientations as being somewhere on a continuum that ranges from 'restraintist' to 'activist.' A 'restraintist' judge was defined as one who believes that precedent, the strict construction of constitutions, and giving deference to legislative intent are extremely important decisional criteria. 'Activists,' on the other hand, were defined as judges who give greater decisional weight to personal attitudes, values, and case outcomes Gibson (1983, 17–18). This operationalization improves upon previous literature in that it allows for an examination of the degree to which role orientations influence judges' voting behavior.

Second, in Chap. 3, this work outlines a method for successfully surveying judges, a group that has been notoriously hard to survey. Mail surveys, though more costly and time–consuming than Internet–based ones, were deemed to be the most effective use of resources, garner the best response rate, and have the lowest potential for non–response bias. Each question was carefully constructed to obtain the desired information while being clear, non–biased, professional, and technically correct. Closed–ended questions were used whenever possible to minimize any potential respondent confusion and provide for clear post–survey coding. The survey design and language was reviewed by faculty at five colleges, an analyst at the Administrative Office of the U.S. Courts, and a research associate at the Federal Judicial Center. Suggestions from these individuals were incorporated wherever possible. Strategies provided by Dillman et al. (2009) for question and questionnaire design were employed whenever possible. This careful construction and implementation of the survey questionnaire garnered an impressive response rate of nearly 39% and may serve as a template for future judicial surveys.

Third, in Chap. 4, this work describes the role orientations of state high court judges. These role orientations were identified by combining judges' responses, on a nationwide mail survey of the entire population of state high court judges, to a series of six statements. The resulting data demonstrates that the judges' role orientations are skewed to the 'restraintist' end of the 'restraintist—activism' spectrum (which ranges from an absolute 'restraintist' score of −9 to an absolute 'activist' score of +9), such that the modal score is −3, the most 'restraintist' judge is −9, and the most 'activist' judge is +2. Despite this skew, the data does resemble a normal distribution.

Fourth, in Chap. 4, this work explores the determinants of state high court judges' role orientations. To do so, three models were constructed to explain the development of judges' role orientations. The first model includes institutional structure variables. The second model includes variables related to the judges' backgrounds. The third model captures the combined effects of both the institutional structure and judges' background variables. Overall, the "Background Model" explains much more of the variation in the judicial role orientation than does the "Institutional Model." This would seem to indicate that a judge's role orientation is formed before the judge joins the bench and thereby limits, but does not eliminate, the effect institutional structures can have on the judge's role orientation. The "Combined Model" outperforms both of the individual models. Standing for reelection or in a retention election, a judge's ideology, and experience as a public defender each exert a consistent and significant influence on judges' role orientations.

Finally, in Chap. 5, this work comprehensively examines how state high court judges' role orientations affect judicial behavior. Operationalizing judicial behavior as a vote to uphold or strike down as unconstitutional a state or local law, a model was constructed that included the judge's role orientation, the degree to which the judge's court has a discretionary docket, and whether the state government was a party to the case. Several variables were statistically significant and had the hypothesized effect. Most important in this research, of course, is the effect that a judge's 'activism' score has on a judge's propensity to strike down state or local laws as unconstitutional. The model indicates that, as expected, the higher a judge's 'activism' score, the more likely he or she is to strike down a state or local law as unconstitutional. In fact, the effect of this variable is that the most 'activist' judge (one with an 'activism' score of +2) is 14.5% more likely to strike a state or local law as unconstitutional as is the least 'activist' judge (one with an 'activism' score of −9).

## 6.2 Summary of the Implications

As noted above, the judge–umpire analogy that began this chapter signals a healthy debate about the proper judicial role orientation, a debate that began long before that day in 2005 and continues to this day. One only needs to look at the flood of newspaper editorials and law review articles that followed Roberts' statements to see its impact.[3] This work has taken no position in the normative debate about the *appropriate* judicial role orientation. Some judges believe that when deciding cases they should consider the implications of their decisions, or consult their own sense of justice. Other judges feel that it should be left up to the political branches of government to fix the implications of their laws, and that the job of judge is merely to apply the law, as written, as unbiasedly as possible. One, from an academic perspective, is no more *correct* than the other.

Indeed, I firmly believe that the debate about which role orientation is *right* and which role orientation is *wrong* should be conducted outside of academia—at the ballot box, in the news and popular media, and in courthouses and legislatures across the country. That being said, it is academia's place to report on what the judges' role orientations are, what effect those role orientations have on judicial behavior, and, once the normative decision is made about what the appropriate judicial role orientation is, academia can provide guidance as to how judges' role orientations are affected by factors such as court structure and judges' backgrounds and professional experiences. In fact, this provides not only an accounting of what state high court judges' role orientations are, but also provides numerous real–world implications for judges' role orientations based on institutional design and judicial selection.

First, how a state structures its judicial selection and retention system can significantly affect the role orientations of its high court judges. The adoption of popular reelection or retention election systems result in an increase in 'activist' judges. And, as 'activist' judges are more likely to strike down a state or local law as unconstitutional, this results in more laws being overturned. This makes sense—few in the public will care whether a judge had to overrule a precedent or strike down an act of the legislature in order to rule in a manner that the public favors. The public cares about results, and the public is responsible for keeping the judges in office; therefore, the judges will care what the public wants. That is, after all, why states choose to subject their judges to popular election. The effect of these systems, as Baum (1994, 751) suggests, is that "judges might try to appeal to the public, in order to ensure reelection."

Also in the realm of institutional design affecting judges' 'activism' is the professionalism of a court. States that have more professional judiciaries, at least when defined by salary, the degree to which the court controls its own docket, and the level of supporting staff that the court has, have a decrease in 'activist' judges. As each of these constituent parts of the court's professionalism score are under the control of state legislatures, states should consider these findings when considering judges' salaries, adjusting courts' jurisdiction, and providing budgetary support. If states want fewer state and local laws struck down as unconstitutional, they might increase salary, increase the discretion courts have in deciding which cases to decide, and increase the support budgets of the courts.

For those charged with choosing judges and concerned about the 'activism' of those under consideration, two factors should weigh most heavily. First, the more liberal a judge is the more likely the judge is to be 'activist.' While the theoretical

[3]See, for example, Liptak (2013).

reasons to support this finding are dubious, the result is persistent across models and consistent with the findings in the judicial role orientation literature. Therefore, if those selecting judges want ones less likely to overturn laws as unconstitutional, they should consider selecting more conservative candidates.

Service as a public defender likewise has a significant effect on the 'activism' of state high court judges. This effect is present both when only modeling the judge's background and when institutional structure variables are controlled for. These findings suggest that a judge who has experience in a public defender's office is less likely to be an 'activist.' Hence, if 'restraintist' judges are desired, judges who have served in the public defender's office should be avoided.

In the final analysis, there are two crucial and overarching implications to this work. First, despite Chief Justice Roberts' assertion, there is no universal judicial role orientation. There exists significant variation in the role orientations of state high court judges, which is to be expected. As theory explains, the process of constructing a role orientation is an individual one based upon preconceived notions, the expectations of relevant others, and the institutional structure within which judges find themselves. Judges will synthesize these components to construct their role orientation, and that role orientation will affect their behavior. Said another way, a judge thinking about what it means to be a 'judge' is not merely a philosophical exercise or a thought experiment. Rather it exerts a significant effect on judicial decision–making.

Second, there are common institutional features, and more significantly, background characteristics and professional experiences of judges, that lend themselves to the development of particular role orientations. Policymakers, or voters, who do not like the role orientations of their judges, or do not like the behavior that these role orientations lead to, are free to either: (1) change the institutional structure of these courts, particularly the judicial selection and retention system and the professionalism of the court; or (2) change the background characteristics and professional experiences they look for in their judges. Certainly, the former is easier to accomplish than the latter, particularly given the proclivity for judicial selection and retention methods to be written into state constitutions. However, salary, discretionary docket control, and level of supporting staff are often within the purview of the state legislature.

## 6.3 Potential for Future Research

Judicial decision–making has long been thought of as some combination of legal, ideological, and strategic considerations. What causes one judge to value one consideration more than another? What causes judges deciding one case to value one consideration more than another? This has been an enduring puzzle in the judicial decision–making literature. This work has sought to provide an theoretically grounded and empirically tested answer to this puzzle using role theory. However, while role theory is well suited for this use, role theory need not be confined to the study of state high court judges. Elements of the theory, conceptualization, and operationalization used in this work could very well be used by political scientists to explore other political actors.

For example, state trial judges who, because of the sheer volume of cases they hear and Americans they come in contact with,[4] are at the forefront of the American legal system. These judges are ripe for further exploration. In the case of state trial court judges, this work's adoption of role theory, its conceptualization of the judicial role orientation as the stimuli that a judge feels should be allowed to influence his or her decision–making, and its operationalization of the judicial role orientation as being on the 'activist–restraintist' spectrum, could all be employed. While surveying the entire population of these judges, given the vast number of them, would be quite difficult, a survey of a reasonably sized sample would be plausible.

Another set of judges for whom this theory, conceptualization, and operationalization of the judicial role orientation might be effective are lower federal judges. While the institutional structure that all federal judges operate under is the same (e.g., life tenure following presidential appointment and Senate confirmation, the same corpus of federal statutory law, etc.), there are many non–institutional stimuli for which there might exist significant variation about whether judges feel they should legitimately be allowed to influence their decision–making. In addition, as there are only 677 U.S. District Court judges (United States Courts N.d.), a population survey would be more easily accomplished than a similar survey of state trial judges. In addition, because more background information is readily available about these individuals, the survey could be brief in length.

One last area of judicial studies that might be able to benefit from components of the theory and conceptualization adopted here is the study of jurors. While being a juror is a short–lived position that people occupy randomly throughout their lives, they occupy this position with no formal or informal training. Jurors often come with few preconceived notions, and function in a very structured environment, yet they have great discretion in reaching their ultimate conclusions. Privacy and legal concerns might make such a study of jurors not possible in some jurisdictions, but it would be fascinating to see the differences in how jurors see their role orientation and how that view affects their decision–making.

Finally, the use of this work's theory and conceptualization need not even be limited to the judiciary. For example, legislative scholars are one group of non–legalists for whom this work might very well serve as an example. Surely, as Chap. 2 revealed, how a legislator sees his or her job surely influences how he or she performs that job. If one were to use the conceptualization of role orientation adopted here, which is the stimuli that legitimately can influence their behavior, the legislative role orientation could be operationalized in a number of ways; for example, how responsive legislators are to the wishes of their constituents, or to leadership, to lobbying efforts, to campaign contributors, etc.

Premised on the idea that how a person conceives his or her position affects how he or she performs that position, the entire breadth of both social and professional positions falls within its paradigm. Given its broad applicability and intuitiveness,

---

[4]Over 103 million cases are filed in state courts each year (LaFountain et al. 2012).

it is unfortunate that political science seems to have moved away from role theory. This work provides just one example of how role theory can be leveraged to explain enduring puzzles in the social sciences it is hoped that this work will help spawn a renaissance in role theoretic examinations of other political phenomena.

## References


Baum, Lawrence. 1994. "What Judges Want: Judges' Goals and Judicial Behavior." *Political Research Quarterly* 47(3): 749–768.

Dillman, Don A., Jolene D. Smyth, and Leah Melani Christian. 2009. *Internet, Mail, and Mixed-Mode Surveys: The Tailored Design Method.* 3rd ed. Hoboken: John Wiley & Sons.

Gibson, James L. 1983. "From Simplicity to Complexity: The Development of Theory in the Study of Judicial Behavior." *Political Behavior* 5(1): 7–49.

Greenhouse, Linda. 2005. "An Opening Performance Worthy of an Experienced Lawyer." *The New York Times,* September 12.

Jackson, Robert H. 1951. "Why Learned and Augustus Hand Became Great." Presented at the Association's Annual Bar Dinner, New York, New York. December 13.

Kerr, Orin. 2008. "Justice Jackson and the Umpire Analogy." August 2. http://www.volokh.com/posts/1217698870.shtml (June 9, 2014).

LaFountain, Robert C., Richard Y. Schauffler, Shauna M. Strickland, and Kathryn Holt. 2012. *Examining the Work of State Courts: An Analysis of 2010 State Court Caseloads.* Washington, D.C.: National Center for State Courts.

Liptak, Adam. 2013. "How Activist Is the Supreme Court?" *The New York Times,* October 12.

McKee, Theodore A. 2006. "Judges as Umpires." *Hofstra Law Review* 35: 1709–1724.

Purdum, Todd S., and Robin Toner. 2005. "Senators to Question 1st Supreme Court Nominee in 11 Years." *The New York Times,* September 12.

*State v. Crittenden.* 1886. 38 La. Ann. 448.

United States Courts. N.d. "Federal Judgeships." http://www.uscourts.gov/JudgesAndJudgeships/FederalJudgeships.aspx (July 29, 2014).

U.S. Congress. Senate. Committee on the Judiciary. 2005. *Hearings on the Nominations of John G. Roberts, Jr. to be Chief Justices of the Supreme Court of the United States.* 109th Cong., 1st sess., 12–15 September.

U.S. Congress. Senate. Committee on the Judiciary. 2006. *Hearings on the Nominations of Samuel A. Alito, Jr., to be Associate Justices of the Supreme Court of the United States.* 109th Cong., 2nd sess., 9–13 January.

U.S. Congress. Senate. Committee on the Judiciary. 2010. *Hearings on the Nominations of Elena Kagan to be an Associate Justices of the Supreme Court of the United States.* 111th Cong., 2nd sess., 1 July.

Zelinsky, Aaron. 2010. "The Justice as Commissioner: Benching the Judge-Umpire Analogy." *Yale Law Journal Online* 119: 113–125.

FSC
www.fsc.org
MIX
Papier | Fördert
gute Waldnutzung
FSC® C083411

Kolibri 360 GmbH
Ferdinand-Jühlke-Straße 7
99095 Erfurt, Deutschland
produktsicherheit@kolibri360.de